# plant partners

# plant partners

## anna pavord

A Dorling Kindersley Book

LONDON, NEW YORK,
SYDNEY, DELHI, PARIS,
MUNICH and
JOHANNESBURG

EDITOR Pamela Brown
ART DIRECTOR Peter Luff
SENIOR MANAGING EDITOR
Anna Kruger
SENIOR MANAGING ART EDITOR
Lee Griffiths
SPECIAL PHOTOGRAPHY
Jonathan Buckley
DTP DESIGNER Louise Waller
PICTURE RESEARCH Anna Grapes
MEDIA RESOURCES Romaine Werblow
PRODUCTION CONTROLLERS
Ruth Charlton, Mandy Inness

First published in
Great Britain in 2001 by
Dorling Kindersley Limited
80 Strand
London WC2R 0RL

Copyright © 2001
Dorling Kindersley Limited
Text copyright © 2001
Anna Pavord

2 4 6 8 10 9 7 5 3 1

A CIP catalogue for this book is
available from the British Library.
ISBN 0751 303550

Reproduced by GRB Editrice, Italy
Printed and bound in Spain by
Graficas Estella

see our complete
catalogue at

**www.dk.com**

# introduction 6

# signs of spring 8

*Early-flowering bulbs, primroses, hellebores
and other plants and planting associations that
help to cast off the shackles of winter,
followed by 10 star plants and their ideal
partners.*

## Star plants

# spring turns to summer 44

*The garden in late spring and early summer,
together with the attributes to look for when
building satisfying plant combinations, followed by
20 star plants and their ideal partners.*

## Star plants

## high summer 110

*Colour considerations, the importance of foliage, and ways of using annuals to keep the garden looking good all through the summer, followed by 20 star plants and their ideal partners.*

Star plants

## into autumn 178

*Organizing an exuberant finale before the frosts come, the splendours of sunflowers and grasses, and some of autumn's unexpected delights, followed by 10 star plants and their ideal partners.*

Star plants

## alternative partners 214

*Other suitable companions for each of the star plants*

contents

THIS BOOK IS ABOUT WAYS OF GROUPING PLANTS in a garden. Sixty star plants are featured in the following pages and each of these stars is presented with a supporting cast – two other plants that will provide the best kind of companionship for it. Sometimes the supporting cast will perform at the same time as the star to give a grand slam, seasonal display. In other groups, companions are chosen to fill in the gaps when the star is "resting", having an off season.

This is the decision you have to make when you are putting groups of plants together in the garden. Are you going for maximum impact, with everything coming out together at a particular time? Or are you planting for continuity, so that whenever you look at a particular spot, something

# introduction

good is happening there? With a little experience, you soon learn who your best friends are, for there are some plants, notably hellebores and euphorbias, that contribute to the garden all the year round. If you include one or two of these "bankers" in your plant groups, you will be more than half way to success.

The best bankers have good foliage because in the end it is leaves, not flowers, that make your garden feel rich, abundant and well-furnished. So in any group in this book, you will find at least one plant which will continue to have point when its flowers have finished. And by choosing plants from each seasonal section, you will ensure that your garden does not run out of steam by the middle of summer. There will be plenty more treats to come.

In this cavalcade of hellebores and hostas, day lilies and irises, tulips and sunflowers, thalictrums and campanulas, you won't find any trees or shrubs. Every garden needs them, to give bulk and presence, as well as shade and a sense of permanence in a plot, but the planting schemes here are made up only of perennials, bulbs, biennials and annuals. In a small garden, there may be room for only one tree, but under and around it you can build up a year-long display of annuals and perennials, mixing and matching the combinations I've suggested in the pages that follow.

Because plants are living things, extremely responsive to factors such as rain or the lack of it, sun, frost and air temperature, flowering times may fluctuate from one year to the next. Aspect also has an effect on performance, as does soil. Heavy clay soils are slower to warm up in spring than light, sandy ones, so plants may be later in waking up. In this book, plants have been nudged into particular seasons, but no-one has told them they have to stick to the plot. The spring season is particularly difficult to predict, as a mild winter or a series of harsh frosts can advance or retard flowering a good deal. Frost might bring a sudden end to your late summer display, too, but these minor hiccups should not prevent you from continually pushing out the boundaries, daring yourself to try something different.

There has never been a time when gardeners have had more plants to play with than we have now. But just *having* them is not enough. The whole point of gardening is to think about our plants' needs and then, by placing them in good company, to make them shine as brightly as they are able.

*Anna Pavord*

### Planning policy

*Tulips and forget-me-nots* (above) *blaze out together in a spring planting. Here, partners are chosen for maximum seasonal impact. There will not be much left to look at in summer or autumn. The combination of primroses with peonies* (above left) *will provide interest over a longer season, for when the primroses have finished, the peony flowers will scarcely have started.*

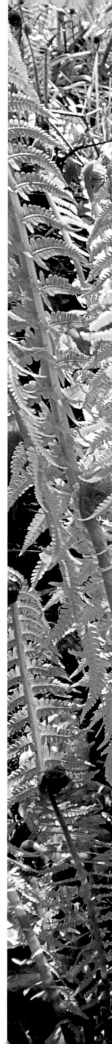

IT IS OF COURSE PERFECTLY POSSIBLE to write lyrical words on the garden in winter: silhouette of trees against the darkening sky, white chalice buds of snowdrop, choir-boy ruffed aconites, all that sort of stuff. But the winter garden. Who needs it? First of all, there's the dressing up: double rations of socks, wellington boots,

# signs of spring

fleece, hat, thick gloves. And that's not allowing for rain. When you open the back door, it is snatched out of your hand by a 75-mile-an-hour gale. There are the pleasures of hail to be remembered, a sensation like being peppered with iced ball bearings. Morosely, you watch the stuff pile up inside the rosettes of foxglove leaves like ice cream in a cornet. You can only stay positive for so long. By the time you have skated over the quagmire of your lawn,

**The year unfurls**

*Leaping up with all the enthusiasm of youth, these shuttlecock ferns (Matteuccia struthiopteris) enjoy the same cool conditions as the dog's tooth violets (Erythronium revolutum) growing with them. Give them dappled shade and they will be happy.*

## Fresh beginnings

*Eagerly awaited by gardeners each new year, the snowdrop, despite its apparent fragility, survives and blooms even in snow. Here the fine* Galanthus 'S. Arnott' *shines out against a backdrop of smudgy Lenten hellebores* (Helleborus orientalis).

viewed the sodden wastes of your borders where rubble seems to be mysteriously bubbling up as if from an underground tip, by the time you have stubbed your toe on an icy edging stone while trying to smell a primrose, you may have decided that the pleasures of the winter garden are only for masochists. The leaves of gunnera, hanging in this season like rhinoceros skins, seem to say the same thing.

The ground could not look more unappealing: heavy, sullen, sticky, cold. The thought of getting your hands in it is as appetizing as dallying in cold porridge. The eye rests on dead fern fronds, the sticks of summer roses and melted puddles of crinum foliage. If you must have a winter garden, make it one that you can plant in summer and then view from the comfort of a centrally heated perch indoors. Any winter effects need to be right outside a window. It is hopeless having winter plantings dotted randomly round the garden where finding them means suffering terminal frostbite and where they sit as lonely as penguins on a broken ice floe.

You might think of bringing winter plants together, for instance under the canopy of a beech or some similar deciduous tree. In winter, when the branches are bare, the ground underneath gets more light and moisture than at any other time of the year. You might start with a big dark *Helleborus foetidus*, even better, a group of them. By adding some big spreads of white snowdrop (*Galanthus*) and yellow aconite (*Eranthis hyemalis*) around their feet, you can imagine quite a pleasant winter scene developing. It would also be a good way of using this kind of ground. It is difficult to get anything special going under big trees in summer, because the earth becomes so dry and shaded. The hellebores, being evergreen, would continue to contribute though, for they are sculptural plants, and you might eventually add small wild daffodils to carry on through the spring, with woodruff or some equally forgiving ground cover to take over later. The woodruff (*Galium odoratum*) has tiny cross-shaped flowers scattered over mats of foliage that is as finely cut as mossy saxifrage.

*Helleborus foetidus*, p.38; *Galanthus* 'John Gray', p.34; *G.* 'Atkinsii', p.96 *Eranthis hyemalis*, p.38

*Galium odoratum*, p.30

For maximum impact, you want groups of plants coming to a peak at the same time in various parts of the garden, but because gardens now are mostly smallish, the schemes also have to go on working, even if in a less concentrated way, for the rest of the year. This is particularly so with groups of winter plants, which is why it is worth persevering with one or

## *The real purpose of winter is to give gardeners the maximum time to look forward to, and dream about, spring.*

two summer additions, without losing sight of the fact that the patch's main contribution will be a winter one. You may find the position too dry for the woodruff, which flowers in late spring and early summer, and reach instead for golden-leaved creeping Jenny (*Lysimachia nummularia* 'Aurea') as ground cover. This is easy and forgiving in less than ideal positions and would put up with the shade cast by big trees in summer.

So it is perfectly possible to conjure something from nothing in the short, dark days at the nadir of the year, but the real purpose of winter is to give gardeners the maximum time to look forward to, and dream about, spring. In the garden, spring means bulbs, as many as you can possibly pack in. This is the explosion we wait for with an impatience that is not equalled by any other event in the garden.

## THE SEASON FOR BULBS

The best thing about bulbs is that, so often, you forget you have planted them. Unlike many garden plants, they keep themselves neatly out of view for most of the time they are not performing. Then suddenly in spring, there they are, not the slightest bit put out that you have not been worrying over them, or making them special snacks. There is a black side to this, of course. There always is. It is the mortifying experience of spearing a dormant bulb through the heart on the end of your garden fork. "I'm so sorry," you say, "I really am," and you rebury the stricken bulb tenderly with some special compost to soothe the wound. But bulbs have enough natural enemies to deal with (mice, birds, slugs, deer…) without their so-called friends turning on them with unkind thrusts.

Crocuses, massed in variety, are one of the most heart-lifting pleasures of an early spring garden. The only problem is that you have to double up like a croquet hoop to admire their finer points, the flush of bronze on the back of the enchanting *C. chrysanthus* 'Zwanenburg Bronze', the brilliance of the orange anthers inside 'Snow Bunting's virginal flower. You also need to choose your moment to admire them. Without sun, they remain resolutely closed while you wait on with the cold damp fingers of winter soil gradually penetrating the soles of your boots.

And, of course, there are mice to be dealt with, for they adore crocuses almost as much as gardeners do. But instead of looking, they eat. The problem was noted almost as soon as crocuses began to be cultivated. An engraving in the *Hortus Floridus*, a nurseryman's catalogue of 1614, shows a mouse nibbling a crocus corm with all the devoted attention of a satisfied gourmet. E. A. Bowles, the famous Edwardian gardener who wrote a classic trio of books starting with *My Garden in Spring*, was a crocus fiend and consequently a psychopath where mice were concerned. "Mice need fighting in all months and by any means," he wrote, and went on to recommend a complicated armoury of cats, poison, slippery jars sunk into the ground, as well as traps baited with brazil nuts. He had some no-nonsense ways with caterpillars as well.

But this was a man who was prepared to wait patiently for 30 years before his cross-fertilization programme produced a pure white seedling of the Greek species *Crocus sieberi*. Such dedication excuses a certain paranoia. Bowles's delight was the species crocus, smaller but earlier flowering than the large varieties, now generally known as Dutch. Both types have their uses, but it is better to plant them in separate places. A bantamweight such as *C. chrysanthus* will be knocked sideways by a heavyweight Dutch such as grey-blue 'Vanguard'.

Since they like the same open well-drained conditions, crocuses fit well with alpine plants such as saxifrages in a scree or rockery and their Lilliputian scale is right for that kind of position. Some of the more vigorous *C. chrysanthus* types will cope in reasonably fine turf, along with early-flowering aconites and colchicums to fill the space in autumn. *Crocus tommasinianus* also grows in grass, provided it is not too rough. The species is a pale lilac colour, which darkens in the selected form 'Ruby Giant'. If you want the crocuses to increase by seeding, as they can, do not mow for at least two weeks after all the foliage has disappeared. The crocus's seed capsule sits almost on the ground and takes some time to ripen and shed its seed.

Choosing varieties is not difficult, once you have decided whether it is blue, white or yellow that you are after. The large-flowered Dutch varieties of *Crocus vernus* or the yellow *C. aureus* are the showiest. But remember that birds tend to attack yellow crocuses more often than white or blue.

*Crocus tommasinianus*, p.202; *C. tommasinianus* 'Barr's Purple', p.106

### Crocus and cyclamen
*In the wild,* Crocus tommasinianus *grows in light woodland, so it will put up with some shade in the garden. It needs sun, though, to open up its flowers and reveal the brilliant orange anthers inside. Here, the crocus is interplanted with pale* Cyclamen coum.

*Crocus vernus* 'Jeanne d'Arc' is the best of the big whites, an elegantly shaped flower with brilliant orange stigmas. 'Striped Beauty' has rich purple markings on a white background. 'Pickwick' has rather larger flowers that are silvery lilac, feathered with purple.

The biggest selection is among the purples – no crocus is truly blue. 'Remembrance', nearly always described as a rich blue, is actually mauve. But it is still an outstanding crocus, as is 'Purpureus Grandiflorus' and the paler 'Queen of the Blues', a refined lavender. Among the early species, you also get more complicated combinations of colour. A clutch of them, such as 'Ladykiller', have handsome deep purple petals, edged with white. The insides of the flowers are surprisingly pure, the slightly bluish white of skimmed milk. There are also some superb varieties streaked with

*Crocus chrysanthus* 'Ladykiller', p.70

## Bulbs rarely have good foliage and benefit enormously when grown among borrowed leaves.

bronze, a combination that does not yet exist among the big crocuses. 'Zwanenburg Bronze' is unusually early, bursting through the ground in a subtle livery of brown on a bright yellow ground.

One of the earliest of the *Narcissus* to bloom, in a tribe that can show flowers for almost three months, is 'February Gold', a cyclamineus type of daffodil that has petals swept back like the ears of piglets fronting a storm. That is very appealing. But it rarely hits the date its name suggests. It usually bobs up unabashed a month later, like a guest turning up for dinner on the wrong night. 'Alliance' is similar. It is early, lasts well and has a particularly determined little trumpet, held almost horizontal to the ground. Try it with golden-leaved feverfew (*Tanacetum*). 'February Silver' came from the same cross, but is a much paler flower, the petals cream, the trumpet a wan margarine yellow.

*Tanacetum parthenium* 'Aureum', p.40

Like crocuses, daffodils generally flower best in full sun, though some such as the Tenby daffodil (*Narcissus obvallaris*) and the wild Lent lily (*N. pseudonarcissus*) grow reasonably well in dappled shade. Narcissi such as the creamy-buff 'Cheerfulness' need a good baking during the summer to instigate flower buds for the following spring. This applies to all the

Tazettas, as this type of narcissus is called. 'Cragford', 'Geranium', 'Scarlet Gem' are all equally prone (poor things) to murder by damp. Try them amongst the emerging foliage of herbaceous geraniums such as *Geranium malviflorum*.

'Minnow' is another Tazetta that needs a hot position for it is from the Mediterranean and used to sunbathing during the summer. 'Minnow' is only about 18cm (7in) high and produces up to four flowers on a single stem, the colour soft yellow, the trumpet slightly darker than the surround. Both 'Minnow' and 'Cheerfulness' need well-drained soil. If yours is heavy, dig in some grit before you plant and set the bulbs on sharp sand in the planting hole. Bone meal helps too, providing nutrients to help develop roots and flowers.

For their smell, you need the old-fashioned Pheasant's Eye narcissus (*N. poeticus* var. *recurvus*). The flowers are elegant and papery, with tiny snub-nosed centres, deep yellow ringed with red. Pheasant's Eye, being a well-proportioned flower, looks good growing in wild areas of the garden. Although its overall style is exactly right for natural situations, it is late, which, if you are planting in grass, can be a disadvantage. When you are choosing bulbs for naturalizing, avoid overbred monsters. They will look as out of place as Madonna at a school coffee morning.

Bulbs that grow in shade are particularly useful though there are not enough of them. The Spanish bluebell, *Hyacinthoides hispanica*, is excellent under trees and amongst the greenery of shade-loving ferns. The flower stem does not droop to one side, like the English bluebell, but stands upright with the flowers ranged all round it, like a rather sparse hyacinth. The white variety is the best, very pure and icy, especially among the newly emerging fronds of shuttlecock ferns or contrasted with the dark leathery foliage of *Euphorbia amygdaloides* var. *robbiae*.

*Euphorbia amygdaloides* var. *robbiae*, p.40

It seeds itself, but not in such a determined manner as our native bluebell, which is a bully in the garden. As well as the white, it comes in various shades of blue, one mid, one dark, and a washed-out pink, which is the least successful colour. The blues are excellent in mixed plantings with late narcissi, such as Pheasant's Eye. Most scillas naturalize easily and are charming components in any spring grouping. *Scilla bifolia* is an intense, bright blue, *S. siberica* a slightly later variety with sky-blue flowers. 'Spring Beauty' is taller, 15cm (6in), and has the pale rather than the bright blue flowers. All are lovely. They are easy to establish and rather

*Scilla bifolia*, p.24; *S. siberica*, p.34

## Chequered charms

*The snake's head fritillary*
(Fritillaria meleagris) *with its
solitary, bell-like flowers needs
neighbours that do not
swamp it. It favours dampish
ground and so is well-
matched with bright blue*
Scilla siberica.

better garden guests than grape hyacinths, which always seem to have too high a proportion of leaf to flower.

All the smaller bulbs – anemone, chionodoxa, crocus, puschkinia and scilla – need planting in sizeable numbers. Use 20 of one kind rather than four or five different kinds. Chionodoxa is closely related to the scilla, but if you look at the stamens, you see that those of the chionodoxa are all held together while those of the scilla fan out separately. In the garden, they like the same conditions and are equally good in half shade. Try them between early hellebores. *Chionodoxa sardensis* is pale blue with a white eye. But is the blue quite as good as the scilla's? No, not really. You might say the same about *Puschkinia scilloides* var. *libanotica* which has pale blue flowers held round the stem like a small hyacinth. The intense blue of the scilla is hard to beat. Try scattering plants round clumps of herbaceous geranium. They hold the space well until the geraniums leaf up properly.

Hyacinths, daffodils, tulips and scillas all flower best when they have been well baked the previous summer but, in a temperate climate, the bakings do not come often enough to realize most bulbs' full potential. Some bulbs – *Tulipa eichleri* (*syn. T. undulatifolia*) for instance – are so gorgeous that you don't want to risk being without them and so, to cover all eventualities, you plant fresh each autumn. *Tulipa eichleri* has brilliant crimson-scarlet flowers, the petals nipping in slightly at the waist and finishing in needle-sharp points. The backs of the outer petals are washed over in greeny buff, so in bud it looks very sober. Then it flings open its petals and reveals itself as the wildly sexy flower it is, set off against leaves that are an elegant greyish green. Try it among clumps of columbines. They will not be in flower at the same time, but the foliage is good on its own at this time of the year, greyish like the tulip's and finely cut.

## PRIMROSES AND OTHER PLEASURES

Some wise gardener once said that the secret of successful gardening was to find out what likes you and then grow a lot of it. So if you have damp, heavy soil, grow plenty of winter- and early spring-flowering primroses. They are useful for filling ground that will be shaded later in the year, for they do not mind that, once they have finished flowering. If you have ordinary primroses in the garden alongside named varieties, you will find all kinds of muddy crosses appearing. Primroses are opportunistic breeders. Of the special kinds, 'Sue Jervis' is a double, a pale, peachy pink that looks good with the clear blue of a pulmonaria or with a variegated brunnera. 'Corporal Baxter' is a deep red double, very luscious and robust. Try it with the wine-tinted foliage of *Helleborus* x *sternii*. 'Miss Indigo' is a startling double blue, with a silvery lacing around the edges of the petals.

*Brunnera macrophylla* 'Hadspen Cream', p.36

*Primula* 'Miss Indigo', p.28

Do not waste double primroses on dry, thin ground. Dig in plenty of compost or even better, manure, wherever they are to grow. Like other classic cottage garden plants, they need chamber pot culture. Grow them where they will be shaded in summer, but not where they will dry out. The plants clump up meatily where they are happy. In order to keep them flowering well, you should split them every other year after they have finished flowering. The simplest way to do this is to ease out the whole clump and pull it apart with your hands. It is quite easy to see where the breaks should come, for the plant arranges itself in a series of crowns, each of which will make a new plant. When you replant, add some bone meal to the soil and do not let the plants dry out.

Wandering round the garden in spring is like being at a party where people you haven't seen for ages suddenly loom into view. You can put a name to them but you've forgotten exactly what they look like and how they talk. Meeting them again gives you a pleasurable sense of rediscovery.

## Working partnership

*Most scillas naturalize easily and are charming components in any spring plantings. The emerging leaves of a spurge provide a dusky backdrop for the scillas' flowers and the whole group is leavened by the silver-splashed foliage of Lamium maculatum.*

*Cyclamen hederifolium,*
p.202

You remember why you liked their company. Or not. The equivalent of the party pooper are weeds such as ground elder, already pushing in around juicy peonies, or leering at verbenas close by.

Many plant groups that give pleasure at this time of year depend on the borrowed foliage of other plants which have yet to flower. Or, in the case of *Cyclamen hederifolium* have already flowered. These are natural companions for spring-flowering scillas. Without the cyclamens' intricately veined leaves around them, scillas are much less telling. Bulbs rarely have good foliage and benefit enormously when grown among borrowed leaves. Try scattering *Scilla bithynica* among the marbled leaves of *Arum creticum*.

You can also use the bronze foliage of early peonies such as *Paeonia cambessedesii* as a backdrop. The leaves of this peony are much finer than the ones of the usual kind of garden peony, most of which have been bred from *P. lactiflora*. They are more pointed, glossier and finished on the undersides with a sumptuous red. The flower isn't as showy as those of the garden hybrids, but it is worth waiting for – mid- to deep pink.

Spurges provide good backgrounds for bulbs too, for the sulphurous greeny-yellow flowers work well with a surprisingly wide range of other colours. Both pink and red tulips look gorgeous in front of a giant spurge such as *Euphorbia characias*. Look for 'Rose Emperor', a Fosteriana tulip described as "cerise", or 'Cantata', another Fosteriana, which is a clear zinging red. 'Prinses Irene' is the right colour to set against spurges too, either bright *Euphorbia polychroma* or the duskier, bronze-leaved *E. x martinii*. If only the arms of the hellebore *H. argutifolius* were more keen on staying upright, that would make a good background for tulips too. The foliage is handsome and the ghostly pale green flowerheads are unselfish enough to play a supporting role behind more flamboyant flowers, but the mature stems have a fatal tendency to crash suddenly to the ground as the new growth erupts from the centre. *Anemone blanda* can cope with the situation though. When crashed on, it philosophically pushes flowers out either side of the obstruction, unfazed, unfussy.

The foliage of ground-covering geraniums hasn't developed enough yet to be of much help, but thalictrum is already good and has the same

**Class act**

*No other flower is as subtle and various as the tulip. Here, where it has been set against the bronze foliage of Euphorbia griffithii, 'Prinses Irene' blazes like a warm fire in mid-spring. Orange dominates, but up the back of each petal run subtle streaks of purple and green.*

## Spears of green

*The leaves of* Crocosmia *'Lucifer' are obliging spring companions, spearing through low mats of the dark-leaved celandine* Ranunculus ficaria *'Brazen Hussy'. By the time the crocosmia starts to flower, the celandines will have dived underground. Sword-shaped foliage whether of iris, crocosmia or gladiolus is an invaluable asset when building up plant groups.*

greyish tones as aquilegia leaves. You could set pale greyish-pink primroses among thalictrums. If that is too twinset and pearls for your taste, add a few clumps of a much darker red-purple primrose. It's like putting on a brilliant slash of lipstick to wake up a sleepy set of clothes.

Ground-covering bugle (*Ajuga*) won't flower until early summer, but the dark, glossy bronze foliage of the variety 'Atropurpurea' will usually set off the blue flowers of some dwarf irises, such as *I. reticulata*. But watch it. Having lulled you into thinking it is a Good Thing, it will then try to strangle the iris. A little bugle goes a long way. While the thin, grassy iris foliage remains above ground, staking a claim to its own *Lebensraum*, you may remember to keep the bugle clear of it. But when the iris foliage sinks under the surface of the soil, the bugle will be over its head in an instant.

Pulmonarias are excellent foliage plants but, at this moment, they are concentrating on flowering. The best leaves come later, when the flowers have finished. In this respect, pale blue *P. saccharata* 'Frühlingshimmel' does

not earn its keep half so well as the much more richly coloured 'Lewis Palmer'. Besides being a better colour, this has more vigorous, upright growth. It goes well with the leathery leaves of Mrs Robb's bonnet, *Euphorbia amygdaloides* var. *robbiae*. Both grow well in shade, provided it is not too dry.

Forget-me-nots will be starting to flower, too, and there are some excellent seed strains with deep blue flowers. Some have a tiny white eye. Try them mixed with a dwarf narcissus such as 'Rip van Winkle'. This does without trumpets entirely and produces a wild double head of two-tone yellow, more like a dandelion with attitude than a daffodil. It is mad, but doesn't realize it. Also mad, but elegantly so, is the two-tone grape hyacinth (*Muscari latifolium*). Instead of the grassy foliage that accompanies the normal grape hyacinths, this emerges with a single broad leaf wrapped around a navy blue flower, finished off unexpectedly with a pale blue topknot. It makes a good companion for the buff double primrose 'Sue Jervis' and *Helleborus* x *sternii*, which has marbled foliage, purple stems, greeny-pink flowers and far too much disfiguring leaf spot. If you are superhuman, you will already have applied fungicide as a preventative spray.

## Tapestry floor

*Variety in form is perhaps the first thing you notice in contrasts of foliage plants, but there are other contrasts to bear in mind, too. Texture, colour, habit, can all make their mark, as in this ground-covering mixture of Lamium maculatum 'Beacon Silver', Ajuga reptans 'Catlin's Giant' and the deeply cut leaves of geranium.*

### BURGEONING LEAVES

Although there is a tumult of flowers in mid-spring – primroses of all kinds, scillas, narcissi, pulmonarias, grape hyacinths, blue-and-white-striped 'Columbine' violas, spurges – it is the great swelling mounds of foliage in the garden that make the whole place look rich and furnished again. Particularly vivid and brilliant at this time is the fountain of growth that comes from the giant fennel, *Ferula communis*, a different group of plants from the fennel you eat, but with the same fine, thread-like foliage. In good soil, this plant will make a fabulous mound of lacy green a metre (3ft) or more across, and perhaps 60cm (24in) high. Then when it feels it has built up enough of a foundation, it sends up a huge flowering stem, topped by flat heads of yellow flowers. But the leaves are its chief glory, though leaf sounds too meaty, too hunky a term for this filigree wirework. Combine it with the spear leaves of a tall iris such as *I. orientalis* and a mound of brunnera, covered now with forget-me-not flowers.

Iris leaves, that is the tall spear-like kind that go with beardless irises such as *I. orientalis* and *I. sibirica*, are very useful at this time of year, acting like exclamation marks among low mounds of geranium leaves or thalictrums. You couldn't use bearded irises like this. They would resent having their rhizomes covered or shaded by vigorous neighbours. But *Iris orientalis* seems to grow anywhere, in sun or shade, the leaves eventually reaching a metre (3ft) in height.

The giant cow parsley (*Selinum wallichianum*) is not such a hypnotically vivid green as the giant fennel, nor as finely cut in its foliage. But the heroic Edwardian gardener E. A. Bowles called it "the queen of the umbellifers", and he never handed out praise lightly. Planted out as a baby, it seems improbable that it will eventually top 1.5m (5ft). Height is a difficult thing to bear in mind when you are placing plants. It is easier to feel their width, to be aware of sideways growth.

The selinum flowers with typical flat umbellifer heads, white rather than yellow, but, as with the giant fennel, it is generally planted for its leaves. Sweet Cicely (*Myrrhis odorata*) is one of the few fern-leaved umbellifers to get its act together this early in the year. The foliage is a wonderfully fresh green, and by late spring it will already be in full flower, heads of greenish, greyish white, not showy, but quite sweet-smelling. The "odorata" tag applies equally to flowers and leaves; they smell of aniseed. It will grow in deep shade where you might partner it with the spotted leaves of pulmonaria and shiny strap foliage of hart's tongue ferns (*Asplenium scolopendrium*). Gerard, one of the early herbalists, said that to eat sweet Ciccly was "exceeding good, holsome and pleasant among other sallade herbes," but perhaps people then were keener on the taste of aniseed. In country areas, the plant was once used as a polish, rubbed into oak panelling and buffed up to a shine when the juice had dried off.

Sweet Cicely is a compact plant, no more than 60cm (24in) high and wide. You wouldn't want it in a starring role, but it is useful because it is early and unfussy about shade. It makes a good backdrop for low mats of

*Asplenium scolopendrium*, p.26

*Although there is a tumult of flowers ..... it is the great swelling mounds of foliage that make the whole place look rich and furnished again.*

*Primula vulgaris* subsp. *sibthorpii* which will be flowering now, short-stemmed pinkish-mauve flowers, each with a yellow eye. This doesn't seed around like the common primrose, but the clumps are easy to split up, once flowering is over.

Variety in form is perhaps the first thing you notice in contrasts of foliage plants: upright iris sword leaves against chunky brunnera leaves, lacy sweet Cicely against the stout, spotty foliage of pulmonarias, but there are other contrasts to bear in mind too, contrasts of texture, of colour, of variegation, of habit. The drooping quality of summer-flowering allium leaves, which grow first up, then turn over on themselves so that their tips touch the ground, is a distinct landmark among the determinedly upright spears of peony foliage, pushing through the ground now with knobby flower buds bossily in place on top. Although you do not think of either alliums or peonies as primarily foliage plants, they are both positive assets in mid-spring. Their real moment of glory will come later when they flower. But how many plants is your garden carrying that contribute little outside their flowering period? Before you pick up any new plant to fill a gap, ask it "So what do you look like when you are not in your best clothes?" And be grateful that the plant can't ask you the same question. □

# Arum italicum 'Marmoratum' *with*
## Astilbe x arendsii 'Irrlicht' *and* Scilla bifolia

The arum is not evergreen, but it starts into growth at a time when most other herbaceous perennials have dived underground for winter. Its growing cycle is a drama in three acts. First comes the superb foliage – the main reason to grow this beauty – each arrow-shaped leaf marbled with silver and edged with a narrow margin of plain green. In spring, the menacing spathe erupts, sheltering an unambivalent spadix. Finally, in a blood-red finale, a berried stalk takes the stage, by which time the leaves have quietly melted away. The astilbe, meanwhile, will have had its own peak, flowering in high summer, when the arum is between acts. The arum's finale is good, but its chief strength is its winter performance. At this stage, of course, the astilbe will have died down, leaving only dark brown flower spikes behind. Do not be in too much of a hurry to cut these down. They are wiry enough to stand upright in winter gales and look wonderful iced glitteringly with frost. The scilla contributes only a short-lived shiver of blue, but it comes when we most want it.

*Arum italicum 'Marmoratum'*
**Height** *15–25cm (6–10in).*
**Spread** *20–30cm (8–12in).*
**Star qualities** *Superb dark green, glossy foliage, elegantly veined in silvery white. The creamy-white spathe is followed in summer by a spike of brilliant red berries.*
**Other varieties** *Arum creticum has showier spathes but less arresting foliage.*

*Astilbe x arendsii 'Irrlicht'*
*The foliage is deeply cut and ferny, providing a lacy underpinning for the summer flowers. These are borne in plumy spikes, crammed with tiny florets which are packed together along the stems. This variety grows to about 60cm (24in). Although astilbes will thrive in sun or shade, they must have moist soil round their feet.*

*Scilla bifolia*
*Scillas will grow anywhere except in the driest and dustiest of soils and, where happy, self-seed liberally. The starry flowers are a soft, purplish blue, borne on stems rarely more than 15cm (6in) high. The leaves have the grace to allow the flowers to perform before they develop fully themselves. Plant bulbs about 7cm (3in) deep and, if you remember, mulch them with leaf-mould or sifted compost in autumn.*

*Arum italicum* 'Marmoratum'

# Asplenium scolopendrium *with* Pulmonaria 'Sissinghurst White' *and* Lunaria annua 'Alba Variegata'

The hart's tongue is unusual among ferns, as the fronds are not divided, but boldly strap shaped, with a rich, glossy finish. Consequently a clump, though arching out in the symmetrical way typical of all ferns, is a meaty landmark in the garden. And it is evergreen, drawing more attention to itself in winter than it ever does in summer. Accentuate the drama of the new leaves uncurling by cutting away all the old foliage in early or mid-spring. Use this group of plants to colonize a shady area of the garden. They will be happy in quite dense shade, provided the soil is not starved or dry. Ferns are so sophisticated, they do without flowers altogether. They are nature's equivalent of the little black dress, accessorized here with lungwort (*Pulmonaria*) and honesty (*Lunaria*). In form, texture and colour the lungwort's foliage contrasts strongly with the hart's tongue's. Honesty provides extra stature and, with its seedheads, a ghostly winter backdrop for the fern.

### *Asplenium scolopendrium* (Hart's tongue fern)
**Height** *45–75cm (18–30in).*
**Spread** *Up to 45cm (18in).*
**Star qualities** *Year-round performance, with evergreen strap-shaped fronds polished as highly as shoe leather. At its best, perhaps, in spring, when the new fronds uncurl, crozier-like, from the furred basal clump.*
**Other varieties** *Capable, like other ferns, of producing many variations on the basic theme: 'Ramocristatum' has fronds that branch like antlers, each one finishing in a flat, frilled crest.*

### Pulmonaria 'Sissinghurst White' (Lungwort)
*All the lungworts make excellent ground-cover plants. They grow strongly, spreading to 60cm (24in), and when in full leaf, between late spring and early winter, smother annual weeds with ruthless ease. The best types, like 'Sissinghurst White', have foliage mottled and splashed with silver. The white flowers appear on 30cm (12in) stems in mid-spring, before the leaves are fully developed.*

### Lunaria annua 'Alba Variegata' (Honesty)
*The name is confusing, as this is a biennial. In the first year it makes a low plant, all leaf and lushness. The following year, it shoots up to flower 75cm (30in) high. The variegation on the leaves of 'Alba Variegata' lessens honesty's coarseness. Although good enough in flower, it is even more useful when the whole plant has been reduced to a bleached winter skeleton, hung with the flat silver discs of its seedheads.*

*Asplenium
scolopendrium*

# Cyclamen coum *with* Primula 'Miss Indigo' *and* Viola 'Rebecca'

These are all low-growing plants to be grouped together in the foreground of a planting. They will do best in soil rich with humus that does not dry out in summer. Primulas, in particular, hate to be baked. Between them, this trio may provide flowers in every month of the year. Much will depend on the primrose's mood. But even if it decides, for once, to stick to its spring schedule, only autumn will be flowerless. Choose carefully among the many varieties of *Cyclamen coum*. Some have leaves as beautiful as any flower and you can cruise happily through autumn on this foliage alone. Give the cyclamen plenty of room and don't let the leaves of either primula or viola droop over them. Both violas and primulas are available in an extraordinary range of colours, so you could plant this trio at intervals along a path, using slightly different colour combinations each time. The crucial word is "slightly". *Cyclamen coum* is a plant that is easily overwhelmed.

### Cyclamen coum
**Height** *10cm (4in).*
**Spread** *5–10cm (2–4in).*
**Flowering time** *Early winter to early spring.*
**Star qualities** *Enchanting, stub-nosed flowers in white or various shades of pink. The best are a deep carmine. Rounded leaves, not as showy as those of* C. hederifolium *(see p.202), and variable in their patterning.*
**Other varieties** *The Pewter Group has leaves heavily overlaid with dull silver;* C. coum *f.* pallidum *'Album' has white flowers.*

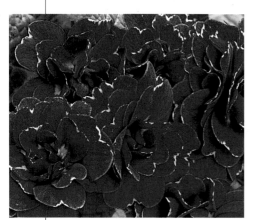

### Primula 'Miss Indigo'
*Primroses are notoriously unreliable clock-watchers. They may let slip flowers in autumn. They may be tempted out to greet a new year. You should certainly have them between early and mid-spring, when the accompanying foliage will be rich, lush green. 'Miss Indigo' has double flowers of a startling blue on stems about 15cm (6in) high. The petals are laced with silver. Split and replant clumps regularly to keep them growing vigorously.*

### Viola 'Rebecca'
*Flat-faced flowers are borne on 10cm (4in) stems above low mats of foliage that spread quickly where they are happy. The long flowering season starts in late spring and continues until late summer. Then you should shear the clumps to the ground so the plants can catch their breath before the next season's show. Deadhead regularly to prolong the flowering season.*

*Cyclamen coum* ▷

# Erythronium 'Pagoda' *with* Cardamine quinquefolia *and* Galium odoratum

A damp, slightly shaded position will suit all these plants, none of which likes to be baked or thirsty. The erythronium has star quality and will catch all eyes when it flowers. But like so many bulbs and corms, it has little to offer when its act is over. That is when you will be glad of the woodruff (*Galium*). Not even its best friend could say it is a star, but it provides an unselfish supporting act. Both foliage and flowers are scented, a bonus that the erythronium cannot provide. Like the woodruff, *Cardamine quinquefolia* is a quiet plant, but it has enormous charm. This trio is well balanced in terms of stature and performance, though the woodruff may try to edge into the cardamine's living space. Don't let it. This is a group chiefly for spring, but the woodruff's foliage will remain fresh and green throughout summer and autumn. Once planted, leave the erythroniums alone. They hate to be disturbed, though they will appreciate an annual mulch of leaf-mould.

### Erythronium 'Pagoda'
**Height** *25–35cm (10–14in).*
**Spread** *15–20cm (6–8in).*
**Flowering time** *Mid- to late spring.*
**Star qualities** *Gorgeous flowers of pale yellow. The petals bend back on themselves, revealing darker yellow stamens inside. Leaves are glossy, faintly mottled, but sparse.*
**Other varieties** *E. revolutum 'White Beauty' has white flowers ringed with brown in the centre; E. dens-canis (European dog's-tooth violet) has pinkish-purple flowers above heavily mottled leaves.*

### Cardamine quinquefolia

*This is a close relative of lady's smock (or cuckoo flower), a wild flower that grows in damp meadows in northern Europe. It has more interesting foliage than lady's smock, as its special name suggests. It hugs the ground closely, providing a mat of leaves from which the pale mauve flowers emerge in mid- and late spring. The flowers will be no taller than the erythronium's.*

### Galium odoratum (Woodruff)

*Mats of bright whorled leaves give the effect of some sprightly moss, topped with tiny, scented white flowers, the four petals arranged in the shape of a cross. Unlike some ground-covering perennials, woodruff is not a bully. Although it will quite quickly spread into a clump about 30cm (12in) across, even at flowering time it is no more than 15cm (6in) high.*

*Erythronium* 'Pagoda'

# Euphorbia myrsinites *with* Tulipa humilis *and* Anemone coronaria

Spring should be grand slam time and bulbs achieve those kinds of effects better than any other kind of plant. But while enjoying these in-your-face displays, you need always to be thinking "What happens afterwards?" You may feel that nothing will ever give you more of a lift than spring-flowering *Tulipa humilis* interplanted with deep blue De Caen anemones. But, nevertheless, something has to happen on that patch for the rest of the year, when both anemone and tulip have dived underground. If you add snaky ground-hugging twirls of grey-leaved *Euphorbia myrsinites*, there will be a splendid sideshow to look at later. The euphorbia flowers at the same time as the tulips and anemones, adding vivid green heads to the mix, so the patch registers as grand slam rather than successional in its planting. But the euphorbia is a good all-round plant, evergreen (or rather evergrey), intriguing, sculptural. On its own, it will make this spot worth visiting long after the bulbs have gone.

### Euphorbia myrsinites
**Height** *5–8cm (2–3in).*
**Spread** *20cm (8in) or more.*
**Flowering time** *Early to mid-spring.*
**Star qualities** *Evergreen, or rather evergrey, perennial, with small pointed leaves carried in spirals around the prostrate stems. Vivid heads of greenish-yellow flowers.*
**Other varieties** Euphorbia cyparissias *has finer, fernier foliage on upright stems. It flowers in late spring, and is invasive, unlike* E. myrsinites. *It is not evergreen.*

### Tulipa humilis
*This is one of the earliest tulips to flower, a small and lunatic species, only 10cm (4in) high. It has a flower of pure, unadulterated magenta, so brilliant that even the designer Schiaparelli would blink at it. On the inside, the magenta is overlaid at the base of the petals with a strange velvety blue-purple and the same tenebrous colour covers the anthers. If the sun shines, the tulips fling caution to the winds and open from globes into wide stars. Such trust.*

### Anemone coronaria
*These are the fat-stemmed, jewel-coloured anemones of florists' shops. The De Caen Group has single flowers, and the St Bridgid has doubles. You can also choose separate colours such as the excellent blue 'Lord Lieutenant', 'The Bride' (right) or 'The Admiral', which is magenta. Each tiny corm will provide as many as 20 flowers in succession, up to 25cm (10in) high. Singles are more free-flowering than doubles.*

*Euphorbia myrsinites*

# Helleborus orientalis *with* Galanthus 'John Gray' *and* Scilla siberica

The Lenten rose, *Helleborus orientalis*, is a particularly useful plant because, although not strictly evergreen, it never leaves a bare patch. The flower buds push through in midwinter and by the time they begin to fade, new leaves have grown up around them. These last, glossily splendid, until the cycle begins all over again the following winter. Any kind of *H. orientalis* is worth having, either the pale ones, with flowers freckled in green, or the deep purple, almost black ones, sinister enough for a witch's brew. The flowers droop on their stems like languid aristocrats. To admire the full complexity of the markings, you must go down on your knees, entirely appropriate in front of this plant. This hellebore is such a bewitching, mesmerizing thing, it will assume the key position in any plant group. Companions such as snowdrops and scillas will not get in the way of its extraordinary flowers. The chalk-white snowdrop will look most dramatic planted between almost black hellebores. Blue scillas will complement white or pale pink hellebores.

## Helleborus orientalis (Lenten rose)

**Height** *45cm (18in).*
**Spread** *45cm (18in).*
**Flowering time** *Late winter to early spring.*
**Star qualities** *Long-lasting flowers in a wide range of colours from white to deepest slate purple. The pale ones are often freckled and speckled inside with darker colours. Handsome, hand-shaped evergreen leaves.*
**Other varieties** *There are more than 60 named varieties. Buy seedling varieties in flower, when you can choose those with the best markings.*

### *Galanthus* 'John Gray' (Snowdrop)

*Eagerly watched for in the chilly days of midwinter, snowdrops are accommodating flowers. If you plant them "in the green", just after they have flowered, they are not difficult to establish. Single snowdrops, such as 'John Gray', with green-tipped flowers swinging from thread-like pedicels, are much prettier things than the bulbous doubles. The doubles look uncomfortable, their petals pulled in too tight at the top. You can almost hear them gasping.*

### *Scilla siberica*

*This species has flowers which are a much purer blue than Scilla bifolia. Look for the variety 'Spring Beauty', which is magnificent, growing 10–15cm (4–6in) tall. Plant the bulbs 5–8cm (2–3in) deep and about 8–10cm (3–4in) apart. Each autumn give them a top-dressing of sifted leaf-mould. Where happy, they self-seed liberally.*

*Helleborus orientalis* ▷

# Hyacinthus orientalis 'King Codro' *with* Brunnera macrophylla 'Hadspen Cream' *and* Narcissus 'Thalia'

The star plant in this group will have absolutely nothing to offer once its spring flowering season is over. But the smell of hyacinths is so rich, so liberating after the deprivations of winter, no spring garden can afford to be without them. 'King Codro' is a rich, deep, saturated blue. When it comes out, the brunnera will be brushed over with the much hazier, paler blue of its own emerging flowers. Hyacinths benefit from a leafy companion to set themselves against, plants which will pick up the baton when the hyacinths' flowers have disappeared. Blue and white hyacinths set among brunnera give the effect of blue and white delft china, very clear and clean. But you could try 'King Codro' with the pale, ferny foliage of sweet Cicely (*Myrrhis odorata*) or plant white ones among dark, leathery *Euphorbia amygdaloides* var. *robbiae*. But stark white hyacinths would look horrible with a creamy narcissus such as 'Thalia', chosen here to complement and reflect the creamy variegation of the brunnera's leaves.

### Hyacinthus orientalis 'King Codro'
**Height** *10–20cm (4–8in).*
**Spread** *6–10cm (3–4in).*
**Flowering time** *Early to mid-spring.*
**Star qualities** *An overwhelming, spicy, rich scent. Short, densely packed spikes of blue flowers, less top-heavy in the garden than on hyacinths that are forced inside.*
**Other varieties** *Flowers may be white, pink, blue, amethyst or pale yellow. 'Blue Jacket' has large spikes of navy blue flowers; 'City of Haarlem' is pale yellow; 'Jan Bos' is deep pink.*

### Brunnera macrophylla 'Hadspen Cream'
*A hearty plant, verging on the coarse, but very generous with its sprays of forget-me-not blue flowers. These last from mid-spring to early summer, but this variety has handsome cream-variegated leaves, which are a great bonus through the rest of the summer and autumn. There is a white-variegated version too, but, unlike 'Hadspen Cream', it burns badly in full sunshine. Coming as it does from Siberia, brunnera is absolutely hardy and trouble-free, too. A clump will spread to about 60cm (24in) with flowering stems at 45cm (18in) tall.*

### Narcissus 'Thalia'
*'Thalia' has no scent. The fault needs to be acknowledged immediately. But the colour is so good, and the habit so engaging, you forgive it this one, glaring oversight. It grows about 38cm (15in) high, with two or three small, delicate creamy-white flowers on a stem. Each has narrow pointed petals and a relatively shallow, frilly cup. It flowers in mid-spring.*

*Hyacinthus orientalis* 'King Codro'

# Leucojum aestivum 'Gravetye Giant' *with* Helleborus foetidus *and* Eranthis hyemalis

Both the snowflake (*Leucojum*) and the winter aconite (*Eranthis*) flower before heavily canopied trees such as sycamore and horse chestnut come into leaf. They will happily colonize places under trees which, though sunny in spring, by high summer may become quite dark and overhung. The hellebore is so used to being ignored it will grow anywhere, though of course it makes bigger, lusher plants where the ground is rich and damp. The snowflake has more by way of foliage than most tubers or bulbs. Already by early winter, the foliage will be showing through, and the freshness of the leaf is a relief when it is set in earth that has been so scoured and beaten by the weather you wonder that anything can turn it to good use again. By the time the flowers come, the clumps of leaves are well established. The winter aconite will flower with the hellebore and the hellebore will hang on to say hello to the first snowflakes, so this is a planting for continuity rather than collision. Where happy, aconites and hellebores self-seed profusely. Over the years, this will change the appearance and emphasis of the group, a process always to be encouraged.

### Leucojum aestivum 'Gravetye Giant' (Snowflake)

**Height** *50–100cm (20–39in).*
**Spread** *10–12cm (4–5in).*
**Flowering time** *Mid- to late spring.*
**Star qualities** *Sheaves of lush, bright green foliage. Flowers like overfed snowdrops, dangling from tall stems.*
**Other varieties** *'Gravetye Giant' is the most robust cultivar of this species. Leucojum vernum has similar flowers but they come earlier (from late winter to early spring) on much shorter stems.*

### Helleborus foetidus (Stinking hellebore)

*If ever a plant needed a name change, this is it. It is impossible for it to sell itself while saddled with such a terrible tag. This is a pity because it is a handsome thing. It holds itself well and in winter and early spring, the dark, evergreen leaves, deeply cut and fingered, are topped with pale green bundles of flower, which last for months. And it doesn't stink at all.*

### Eranthis hyemalis (Winter aconite)

*Aconites are one of the earliest bulbs to flower, racing neck and neck with snowdrops to appear in late winter. Fat juicy stems, 5–10cm (2–4in) long, end in ruffs of bright green leaves which surround the globe-shaped flowers. The tubers hate to be dried out. Try to get hold of plants "in the green", just after they have finished flowering. Planted like this, they will establish much more easily than from dry tubers.*

# Narcissus 'Quail' *with* Tanacetum parthenium 'Aureum' *and* Euphorbia amygdaloides var. robbiae

Make the most of 'Quail's powerful spring scent. When it has gone, there will be nothing else in this group to match it. Fortunately, it dies well, because its leaves are dark and grassy, not in any way an eyesore in decay like the leaves of monster-sized daffodils. There are two useful "bankers" here to set off the lovely 'Quail' when it comes into flower and to hold the patch together when it has gone. The sober, dark spurge (*Euphorbia*) is an excellent colonizer, though it has a mind of its own as to where it puts itself. It thrives in a wide range of conditions, including deep shade, but appreciates a mulch of compost in spring. Cut out dead stems as necessary and keep an eye on its wandering feet. It is lovely with daffodils, which contrast both with the sombre foliage and the lime-green tones of the spurge's flowers. You will need to edit the group periodically, pulling up spurge where it is not wanted and transplanting or reducing new young seedlings of feverfew (*Tanacetum*).

### *Narcissus* 'Quail'

**Height** *35cm (14in).*
**Spread** *10–12cm (4–5in).*
**Flowering time** *Mid- to late spring.*
**Star qualities** *A superb scent, like all the jonquils. There are several flowers to a stem, the petals and cups both the same rich, thickly-textured golden yellow.*
**Other varieties** *Narcissus jonquilla, the species from which all the jonquils spring, is charming, shorter than 'Quail'; 'Trevithian', another jonquil, has flowers of soft primrose.*

### *Tanacetum parthenium* 'Aureum' (Golden feverfew)

*This is a short-lived perennial at best, never growing more than 30cm (12in) in any direction. But it is an enthusiastic self-seeder, so the problem will not be in keeping it, but in curbing it. On dull foggy days in winter, young plants shine out like beacons, low mounds of rich golden foliage. It is undemanding, which means that it is underrated. Its white daisy flowers (they come in summer) can be sheared off, if they dissipate the look you are after.*

### *Euphorbia amygdaloides* var. *robbiae* (Mrs Robb's bonnet)

*This evergreen perennial spurge is an excellent colonizer for semi-wild areas in the garden, but is handsome enough to be used in a border as well. The leaves make dark, leathery rosettes and in spring there are long-lasting heads of lime-green flowers. It grows about 30cm (12in) high and is a wanderer, spreading by underground stolons.*

*Narcissus* 'Quail'

# Tulipa 'Prinses Irene' *with* Geranium x riversleaianum 'Mavis Simpson' *and* Euphorbia polychroma 'Major'

The second half of spring should be awash with tulips in quantity. If you have heavy, sticky ground, the kind of situation that tulips hate, plant them in simple plastic pots (but big pots) and drop them into position behind the mounds of euphorbia foliage. Foliage of many plants such as oriental poppies, fennel, geraniums and peonies is tall enough to disguise the containers themselves by the time tulips want to flower. The particular limy yellow-green of this euphorbia looks wonderful with orange tulips such as 'Prinses Irene' (though in fact it's far too subtle a tulip to be labelled as orange). Brilliant red tulips would be equally good. Yellow may get swallowed up in the yellowness of the spurge. When this dazzling display is over, the geranium will get into gear and provide flowers all the way through until autumn, especially if you remember to shear back stems after the first flush of flowers.

### Tulipa 'Prinses Irene'
**Height** *30–35cm (12–14in).*
**Spread** *10–12cm (4–5in).*
**Flowering time** *Mid-spring.*
**Star qualities** *Gorgeous markings of purple and hints of green streak and flame the soft orange petals. A remarkable tulip with pale green stigma, yellow stamens and olive-green anthers.*
**Other varieties** *'Annie Schilder' has deeper orange flowers; 'Yokohama' is yellow with a thin, pointed bud, very elegant; 'Roulette' has blood-red flowers, several to a stem.*

### Geranium x riversleaianum 'Mavis Simpson'
*All the geraniums derived from this hybrid make semi-evergreen, clump-forming perennials with rounded, greyish-green leaves. Flowers are borne over a long period from early summer to autumn. 'Mavis Simpson' has clear, light pink flowers with pale centres. 'Russell Prichard' is similar, but has deep magenta flowers. Each plant may spread to cover a square metre of ground, but is scarcely 30cm (12in) high.*

### Euphorbia polychroma 'Major'
*This easy spurge makes a soft, rounded hummock of leaves about 50cm (20in) high and wide. It behaves like a true herbacous perennial, unlike its bigger cousin, shrubby E. characias (see p.80). The disadvantage of this is that it leaves a gap in winter. But it has wonderfully intense flowers, an almost fluorescent greenish yellow, which are not actually flowers at all but bracts supporting insignificant flowers above. These last from mid- through to late spring.*

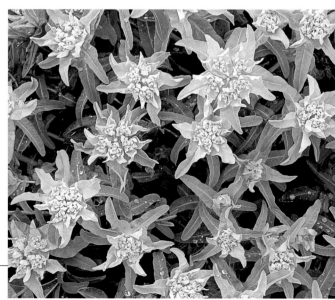

*Tulipa* 'Prinses Irene'

FOR A GARDEN THAT IS TO SATISFY YOU in the long term you need to look further than flowers. Think of them as extras, the icing on the cake, and assess plants by other qualities instead. What sort of habit does the plant have? What are its leaves like? Are they well shaped? Do they have texture? It is by manipulating all these

# spring turns to summer

attributes that you build up the best plant groups in a garden. Of course, flower colour has a part to play too, but it is by no means the most important consideration. Take epimediums. They are in flower at this time of the year, white sprays on *E. grandiflorum* 'Nanum', crimson on *E. x rubrum*, clear yellow on *E. davidii*. The flowers are

### Shades of refreshment
*Lime green, though a vivid, arresting tone, mixes well with any other colour you set beside it. Here it comes from Smyrnium perfoliatum. This is biennial, so the flowers come in the second year. Forget-me-nots enjoy the same kind of conditions and make natural companions.*

## Texture and form

*Ferns such as this shuttlecock type* (Matteuccia struthiopteris) *are so confident of their beauty, they do without flowers altogether. Its elegant vase shape contrasts well with the tough, hand-shaped leaves of* Rodgersia podophylla.

*Epimedium* x *perralchicum*, p.72

enchanting (though small). They grow on strong, thin wiry stems well above the foliage. They are delicately made, four rounded inner petals curving down, four strappy outer ones making a ruff round them. But by the end of the month the flowers will be finished. What can the epimedium offer then to earn its place in the garden for the next 11 months? Plenty, for it has superb leaves. They are held, often in arrangements of three, on thin stiff stems. The leaf at the top of the stalk is symmetrically balanced, the pair that face each other lower down are lopsided, the outer lobe of each pulled as if by gravity towards the ground.

The new leaves will be almost fully formed by the time the flowers finish, replacing the old foliage that has lasted through the winter. On *Epimedium* x *rubrum* the green is edged and smudged with mahogany. The shape and colour of the foliage, the high gloss on the leaves of some varieties, make epimediums good mixers. They work well among clumps of cyclamen, another plant that has leaves at least as important as its flowers. They also sit comfortably among hellebores, particularly the hand-shaped leaves of *H. orientalis*. But of course, to get these sumptuous effects, you have to provide the conditions that epimediums (and cyclamen and hellebores) enjoy: cool, moist soil with plenty of humus in it.

### THE GENTLE MADNESS OF FERNS

Ferns are confident enough to dispense with flowers altogether. Form is all and, undistracted by colour, you can settle to the engrossing business of finding them suitable partners. Set unfurling fronds of the common male fern, *Dryopteris filix-mas*, behind low spreading masses of silver-leaved lamium: uprights and horizontals. Use shuttlecock ferns (*Matteuccia struthiopteris*) between clumps of the fat-leaved saxifrage, *Saxifraga cortusifolia*: lace and polished leather.

*Matteuccia struthiopteris,* p.152

*Ferns do not tug at your shirt as you walk by them. They just get on with being ferny and wait for you to notice what they are about.*

Willy-nilly, ferns turn you into a collector because without any prompting, they try out such a huge variety of dotty tricks. They suddenly produce flourishes like bunches of parsley at the ends of their leaves. They subdivide wildly to make leaf patterns more complex than the Amazon delta. A seemingly sensible, law-abiding fern such as the hart's tongue (*Asplenium scolopendrium*) will suddenly flip its lid and perm the edges of its leaves into a series of frilly curves, or experiment with a black stem instead of a green one. Symmetry is built into them, so even if a fern is being lunatic, it is graceful with it. Grace is perhaps a fern's most important attribute, but it is a quiet one. Ferns do not tug at your shirt as you walk by them. They just get on with being ferny and wait for you to notice what they are about.

*Asplenium scolopendrium,* p.26

All ferns prefer some shade but the golden male fern, *Dryopteris affinis*, and the soft shield fern, *Polystichum setiferum*, will put up with the sun, especially if you can mulch to keep their roots cool. Try them with pink

*Polystichum setiferum* 'Pulcherrimum Bevis', p.96

opium poppies or a tall yellow primula, such as *P. florindae*. The big family of polypodys is equally obliging. The common polypody, *Polypodium vulgare*, will sow itself along the arms of old fruit trees or colonize the risers of a step. After a week or so with no rain, the fronds frizzle up completely, but then, like Japanese paper flowers dropped in water, they leap up again at the first wetting. Where ferns colonize walls in the garden, they usually choose the north face.

To get the full drama of the ferns' uncurling, cut away the old dead fronds before the show starts. They all have slightly different ways of performing. Only the acrobatic shield ferns, the polystichums, have mastered the tricky art of the back flip. Zen gymnastics.

## THE IRIS CALENDAR

Sword-shaped leaves are great allies in mixed plantings, separating the rather sleepy, rounded clumps that so many herbaceous perennials grow into. You might for instance reach for the obliging *Iris orientalis*. The flowers, white with yellow throats, appear in early summer, but by late spring the leaves will already be 90cm (36in) high, spearing through mounds of thalictrum, giving backbone to a rather spindly achillea, supporting a hummock of autumn-flowering sedum. This iris is a plant that, like the best sort of aunt, can get along in any sort of company. The very similar Monspur irises, which also belong to the Spuria group, can be used in the same way. They make large clumps, with the same strong upright leaves as *I. orientalis*. The flowers are blue, shaped like the old fleur-de-lys. Use them with campanulas and lupins.

Where you want to create the same sort of effect on a smaller scale, use an iris such as *I. pallida* 'Variegata', which holds its leaves, like a bearded iris, in flat, two-dimensional fans. They are broad, glaucous and, in this variety, striped with rich cream. The flowers are pale blue. It will provide a linking element between, say, the last stragglers in a patch of jonquils and the first flowering of a group of deep purple aquilegias. It also looks lovely

set in the midst of love-in-a-mist's ferny foliage.

All these irises sulk when moved. They need time to settle. The Spuria types are best planted in autumn, with the rhizomes set no more than 5cm (2in) deep in well-worked soil to which you have added some bone meal. *Iris pallida* needs more sun and you can plant this in summer, with the top of the rhizome sitting above the ground where it can get baked.

With some careful trawling among the catalogues, you can have irises in bloom for seven months of the year. You would start with the little bulbous ones such as the Turkish *Iris histrioides* or *I. reticulata* from Russia and the Caucasus, which would see you through late winter and early spring. You also would not want to be without another winter-flowerer, the Algerian iris, *I. unguicularis*, which thrives in poor soil at the base of a hot, sunny wall.

In mid-spring you would expect to see the first of the dwarf bearded irises, types bred from the European species *I. pumila*. You would coast through late spring with different types of Dutch bulbous iris. These are the ones that you see for sale in thin sheaves in florists' shops, a promise of things to come when the weather outside is about as hideous as it can get. If you plant these bulbous irises in the garden in autumn, though, late spring is their most likely flowering time. They take up very little room and are extremely useful for slipping between clumps of herbaceous

### Damp delights

*Siberian irises such as this* Iris sibirica *'Placid Waters' grow best in moist soil in full sun, conditions which also suit the golden-leaved sedge,* Carex elata *'Aurea', behind it. The papery flowers of* Astrantia major *'Roma' contribute long-lasting interest to this group of plants.*

# *Choosing plants to set together.....*
# *is not a process that should keep you*
# *awake at night, worrying.*

perennials, geraniums, astrantias, campanulas, which at this stage are not too leafy to overpower them. The iris foliage is thin and grassy and when it has flowered the whole plant disappears underground, just like a daffodil.

But early summer is the time when irises explode. It is the season of the magnificent great bearded types, with poker stiff stems and fans of grey foliage. The beardless *Iris sibirica* also flowers now, not so showy, but a great deal easier to use in mixed plantings. And there is the delicious dwarf species *I. graminea*, with red-purple flowers smelling of ripe plums. This is ideal for patches at the front of a sunny border, as the grassy leaves are at most only 30cm (12in) high. Try it with the beautiful Pasque flower, *Pulsatilla vulgaris*, and aquilegias.

Iris flowers, models of symmetry, are built in threes: three outside petals, called falls, three upright petals, called standards, and right in the centre, three strappy petals called style arms protecting the anthers. The beards of the bearded iris make hairy tufts down the centre of the falls. These are the showiest of all the irises, but not the easiest to place in the garden. They need full sun for at least half the day and they do not like other plants flopping over their rhizomes. The lighter your soil, the easier you will find them. Alkaline soil is better than acid.

The bearded irises range from dwarf – no more than 15cm (6in) high – to tall, which can be at least 1.2m (4ft). Modern breeding has brought about some spectacular flowers, frilled and ruffled, but it seems also to have made new bearded irises more susceptible to disease. Leaf spot is one of the worst. It usually appears just after flowering, small, round, brownish-grey spots which spread at an alarming rate. First the tips of the leaves wither, then the entire leaf collapses. Spraying with a fungicide helps, but you need to start before flowering and continue every 10–14 days.

The French painter Claude Monet adored irises and in his famous garden at Giverny tall bearded irises are set in strong, long lines down the edges of a sequence of narrow beds. These beds are heaped up into long

Bearded iris: *Iris* 'Jane Phillips', p.84

*Iris sibirica*, p.86

*Pulsatilla vulgaris*, p.98

## Fine alliance
*Bearded irises are not always easy to use in mixed plantings. If they are to flower well, the sun needs to ripen the rhizomes from which they grow. But some annual flowers such as love-in-a-mist (Nigella damascena) are light and airy enough to enhance the irises' performance, without ever getting in the way.*

mounds, like asparagus beds, and the garden itself is open and unshaded. This is what the bearded irises like: good drainage at the roots and plenty of sun to ripen the rhizomes. For the authentic Giverny effect, use irises with lambs' ears (*Stachys byzantina*), forget-me-nots, purple tulips, mauve sweet rocket, tall wobbly alliums, dark purple wallflowers, aubrieta and opium poppies. But remember that the irises thrive at Giverny because they are planted on the edge of Monet's narrow beds, where the foliage of other plants does not flop over them. They are not good sharers. If you plant them in mixed beds or borders, keep them, likewise, to the front, so that the rhizomes are open to light and sun.

Choosing plants to set together in the garden should be the best, the most enjoyable part of making a garden. This is not a process that should keep you awake at night, worrying. If you choose plants carefully in the first place, combinations containing them will work more often than not. Some groups of plants such as irises, violas, tulips, peonies and alliums are breathtaking enough to transcend any surrounding disasters. You can enhance their beauty with thoughtful companion planting, but you cannot diminish it, however hard you try.

## FRIENDLY FACES

It is very much easier to love plants (and people) if they show some sign of loving you in return. To get violas on your side, give them heavy, damp ground. You may find that they grow better in half shade than they do in sun. All the violas have five petals, two making rounded ears at the top, two making cheeks at the sides and one pouting into a chin at the bottom, but the way that the petals are put together gives each variety a completely different character. Some are moon-faced, the petals running together into a gentle rounded shape. Others have narrower petals that make long rather peaky faces, as with the superb 'Ardross Gem'.

*Viola* 'Ardross Gem', p.106

This viola spreads out a low mat of foliage before raising its flowers well above the leaves on wiry 18cm (7in) stems. This gives quite a different effect from the violas that like to have their leaves about them when they flower and pull their foliage up around their necks like shawls. Try 'Ardross Gem' with a silver-leaved mossy saxifrage and a dwarf pink geranium, such as *G. sanguineum* var. *striatum*. It will grow well in a pot, though not quite as luxuriantly as it does in open ground. The mat of leaves spreads to cover the soil and stops it drying out and the flowers bob about in the space

above. Do not plant a viola in a pot smaller than 18cm (7in). It will dry out too quickly. Nor should the pot be in full sun. But violas look good next to monochrome potted succulents such as aeoniums and echeverias.

The colours of violas are generally smudged, the blues always on the purplish side, the yellows often overlaid on the backs of the petals with purple, which sucks the intensity out of the primary colour. Few of the flowers are pure selfs, that is, the same colour all over. Even 'Nellie Britton' (*syn.* 'Haslemere') which seems to be a uniform dirty mauve–pink – a phenomenal colour – has got dark-rayed whiskers leading to a tiny yellow eye.

'Nellie Britton' is good with the foliage of a hellebore such as *H.* x *sternii* 'Boughton Beauty'. Both enjoy the same kind of growing conditions and both have been painted from the same palette, the weird pink of the viola appearing in a deeper shade on the stems of the hellebore. 'Vita' is similar, a shade browner perhaps. Violas are easy garden plants, because they are reasonably tolerant in terms of growing conditions and make accommodating companions for plants that, as with hellebores, have a

## Dear Molly

*Although not the easiest viola to grow well, 'Irish Molly' is one of the most desirable, with flowers of an extraordinary khaki colour. The frothy lime-green heads of* Alchemilla mollis *pick up and accentuate the strange green hidden in the viola.*

*Colchicum agrippinum,*
p.206

completely different flowering season. They can, for instance, usefully disguise the collapsing foliage of colchicums, which are looking at their worst by late spring. But the colchicums' time will come just when you shear back the violas for their winter rest and the one show will drift seamlessly through to the next. Or should. It is difficult to force yourself to chop the viola and waste its autumn flowers, but it is the only other job besides the deadheading that is vital to keep the plants on their feet.

The fact that you can never quite describe the exact colour of any particular viola is an advantage. Their smudgy colours, like chameleons' skins, adapt to whatever company they find themselves in. The silvery mauve flowers of 'Maggie Mott' look cool with grey artemisias, but

> *If slugs ate bindweed, it would be much easier to believe that we are indeed part of some Grand Design.*

change their character completely when combined with the warmer shades of verbenas. Maggie Mott lived at a house called Scotswood in Sunningdale, Berkshire, where her family had a gardener who was a viola fancier. He named a seedling after his employer's daughter and showed it successfully at the Royal Horticultural Society. It appeared in the Society's viola trials in 1904 and has been in cultivation ever since.

It flourished in India in the 1930s when the garden designer John Codrington used it in the gardens of the Residency in Delhi. The Commander in Chief, Sir Phillip Chetwode, had grandiose ideas for a large circular pool at the end of a vista there. The pool proved too expensive a project so Codrington planted a huge circle of 'Maggie Mott' instead, the silvery colour giving the illusion from the Residency windows that there really was water at the end of the view.

The darkest of all the violas, perhaps the blackest of all flowers, is 'Molly Sanderson', which has petals with the sheen of viciously expensive satin. It is not as easy to place as other violas. A little time ago there was a vogue (fortunately brief) for all black gardens, when you saw 'Molly Sanderson' combined with grassy black ophiopogon and dark chocolate-scented cosmos. None gained in the association. Nor should you be tempted to use this dark, saturated shade with white-flowered plants such as the low-growing *Achillea* 'Huteri'. The contrast is too obvious. Try it instead with the misty blue of a veronica such as 'Spode Blue' or 'Ionian Skies', or the magenta of a verbena.

When you are planting violas, think cool, think damp. They will not flourish in the dry shade under trees, nor will they be happy in light soil in full sun. Mulching around plants improves them wonderfully, for it retains moisture in the soil and keeps the roots cool. Liquid feeds help too, particularly in bolstering up plants after you have sheared them down in autumn. Unfortunately slugs have a great fancy for violas, a fatal flaw in the so-called balance of nature. If they ate bindweed, it would be much easier to believe that we are indeed part of some Grand Design.

### OF TULIPS AND WALLFLOWERS

No garden can have too many tulips. This is one of the few infallible rules in gardening. There are thousands of varieties to choose from, but for some of the most interesting ones, look in the groups called Lily Flowered and Single Late (the Single Lates are sometimes labelled Cottage tulips). There's a lot of old blood coursing round in these groups and the flowers sometimes do surprising things, throwing back to colours and forms that we never normally see. Try 'Alabaster', a pure white flower that has been around since at least 1942. Nobody knows who raised it, which is always a good sign. It suggests age and the oldest flowers are often the most graceful. It grows to about 60cm (24in) and flowers in late spring. Try 'Vlammenspel', a sport of the superb old English tulip (no longer available) called 'Inglescombe Yellow'. This sport is a yellow tulip, feathered and flamed with orange and red, and grows to about 50cm (20in). Try the Lily Flowered tulip 'White Triumphator' with yellow doronicum or a cloud of blue forget-me-nots.

*Tulipa sprengeri*, p.104

Get into the habit of having a back-up supply of crowd-pulling tulips, which you can grow in plain black plastic pots and then drop into any bare bit of bed or border. By mid- to late spring, foliage is growing fast, so peony leaves, campanulas or fennel soon disguise the pots themselves, in any places where they need disguising. You might try, for instance, bringing in pots of the superb tulip 'Blue Parrot' to complement the restrained and handsome foliage of the hosta 'Krossa Regal'. This has greyish leaves, but the stem grows unusually long before the elegant,

*Hosta* 'Krossa Regal', p.164

### Deeper and deeper

*Purple is one of the richest colours that a gardener can use and tulips provide purple in plenty. Combined on their own with blue forget-me-nots, the effect would be rich and sombre, but the scene here is enlivened by an underplanting of cream-coloured wallflowers.*

not-too-broad leaf begins to develop. The plant stands high and urn-like. Pots confer another advantage. If your ground is heavy, very sticky clay (in a word, hideously unsuitable for bulbs), pots allow you to arrange drainage – critical for so many bulbs – more easily: 2–3cm (1in) of sharp grit at the bottom, then compost, the bulbs settled comfortably into this bed, then covered with more compost. It's much easier than trying to burrow holes into some clay maw, some vortex of stickiness which you know is going to be a coffin for bulbs designed for ground as fast draining as a sieve. A bulb planter, which works well when you are planting in grass, is not so useful in open ground, where the plug of earth that you draw out tends to crumble to bits.

Some pots are for display, but for plunging into gaps you can use simple, cheap black plastic pots. It's not worth using anything smaller than 30–35cm (12–14in) across, because you can't then stuff in enough bulbs to make a splash in a border. You can use your own home-made compost, unsieved, in the bottom half of the pot, where the bits of stick and stalk will help with the drainage, then put sieved compost on top of the bulbs. To discourage birds and slugs, finish off the pots with a top-dressing of gravel.

If purple is the theme, tulips will give it to you in vast variety. 'Negrita' is a star, a Triumph or mid-season tulip, with a habit of throwing more than the usual six petals, so the resulting flowers are astonishingly full and blowsy. It grows to about 45cm (18in) and flowers in late spring. 'Purple Prince' is another winner, slightly earlier and shorter than 'Negrita' but with the same rich, lustrous colour. Only occasionally does this wondrous family disappoint. 'Dreaming Maid' is a wishy-washy colour, a small, greyish-mauve flower that weathers badly. The base of a tulip can often redeem an otherwise undistinguished flower, but even this is boring: pale and indeterminate with pale creamy stamens. And 'Arabian Mystery', described as "a wonderful rich violet–purple, silvery white at edge of petals" is a dog's breakfast. The silvery edging makes the flower look as though it is sick, or bleaching badly in the light. It does not work. But there are few duffers, and they are effortlessly eclipsed by marvels such as purple 'Bleu Amiable'. Use it with the Lily Flowered tulip 'China Pink'

### Bravura performance

*Two reddish-orange Lily Flowered tulips, 'Dyanito' and 'Ballerina', are used to stunning effect against a backdrop of Euphorbia x martinii. Having mediocre foliage themselves, tulips look best where they can borrow leaves from other surrounding plants.*

## Mahogany and lace

*Smudgy tones of tan, maroon, mahogany and toffee are the wallflower's great contribution to the late spring garden. Few other flowers provide such a strange, enigmatic palette of colours. Feathery fronds of fennel set them off to perfection.*

*Tulipa* 'Prinses Irene', p.42

among forget–me–nots, variegated honesty and elegant *Gladiolus tristis*.

But of all the purples, 'Blue Parrot' is the best, not blue at all of course, since it is one of the few colours that a tulip cannot produce. It is not even wildly parroty, compared for instance with the crazy 'Weber's Parrot'. Its petals curl in on themselves, making a somewhat congested flower. The colour is good: old–fashioned Victorian purple, which also runs down the top part of the flower stem. The leaves are narrowish and pointed, well proportioned in relation to the flower. This is not always the case with tulips, some of which have foliage that is much too meaty. The base, hidden under the curling petals, is a surprising peacock blue. This is a handsome, elegant, classy tulip which comes into flower in late spring. You may find it zooms straight into the category of Tulips You Cannot Possibly Live Without. Red 'Cantata', creamy 'Magier' and orange 'Prinses Irene' should be there too.

Tulips are natural companions for wallflowers, and though wallflowers are often badly used, they are never hackneyed. Their rich tawny colours consort well with both tulips and daffodils and the smell, when a warmish shaft of sun tickles their scent glands, is a glorious antidote to the sloth brought on by winter hibernation. A late spring garden should be

*It is one of the few infallible rules of gardening that no garden can have too many tulips.*

swooning with more scents than a seraglio and one sniff of a wallflower can open up a whole Pandora's box of emotions: rows, reconciliations, a particular meal, a birthday party. A garden without smells would be a hamstrung thing.

The precise smell of a wallflower is not easy to conjure up. Spice is it? But which spice? It is odd that a smell so memorable when present should be so elusive when past. Poor wallflower! And we always think of it in terms of rent-a-crowd, never as a solo star. One wallflower is a ludicrous proposition. Daffodils, which suffer from the same difficulty, at least had a poem written about them. You have to use wallflowers en masse. They are not in themselves beautiful objects, though if you have room to allow them to become the perennials that they are by nature, they develop into rather venerable, sprawling plants, good when seen flopping over the edge of a raised terrace bed, or best of all, out of a crack in a stone wall. If badly grown, they are leggy, scraggy things, but they have the potential to be outstanding. There is that smell, and a wonderfully subfusc range of colours, rich mahogany as well as pale cream, dirty purple and glowing ruby. There is a mixture called 'Persian Carpet' which exactly describes the effect wallflowers give. You can also get separate colours.

If you are planting them with bulbs, plant wallflowers first, bulbs after. Then you will not accidentally spear bulbs hidden underground. If you are buying wallflower plants rather than growing your own, remember that what you buy in autumn is what you will see in spring. If you buy measly plants, they will still be measly though in flower in spring: no extra growing takes place during winter. Look for plants that have rounded

**Harmony of spheres**

*Long after these fine purple irises have disappeared from the scene, the globe heads of Allium hollandicum 'Purple Sensation' will continue to delight the eye. Colour gradually bleaches out of them but on their strong stems, the ghostly straw-coloured baubles will last until winter.*

well-developed heads of foliage rather than single stems and get them into the ground as soon as you can. Height depends to a certain extent on variety. Standard wallflowers grow to about 45cm (18in), but there are various dwarf strains with names such as 'Tom Thumb' that are considerably shorter and useful if you are trying to get the essence of the season in the space of a windowbox.

Along with stocks and sweet Williams, wallflowers are archetypal cottage garden plants. The bedding craze of the nineteenth century brought them into grander homes, but they have never been looked on as smart plants. Today's plant snobs may spurn 'Persian Carpet' and its kind and instead search out plants of 'Bloody Warrior' with oxblood-red double flowers set rather far apart on the stem. The special wallflowers 'Bloody Warrior', 'Harpur Crewe' (a double yellow), 'Baden-Powell' (smaller, but otherwise

*One sniff of a wallflower can open up a whole Pandora's box of emotions: rows, reconciliations, a particular meal, a birthday party.*

much the same) and the wallflower-like *Erysimum* 'Bowles' Mauve' (blue-grey foliage and soft purple flowers) are later to come into flower than the common sorts grown from seed which flower from mid-spring to early summer. The specialities won't start until late spring. Wallflowers are sociable plants. Try 'Primrose Monarch' with pale blue pansies (or black violas if you are looking for a more dramatic contrast). For the authentic Monet effect, use clear yellow wallflowers with forget-me-nots. Enhance the rich mahogany shades with tulips such as brownish 'Abu Hassan' or the elegant Lily Flowered 'Queen of Sheba'.

## CELESTIAL PEONIES

Old-fashioned, late-flowering Cottage tulips also consort well with old-fashioned peonies, the deep crimson, double-flowered kind. The flowers are named after Paeon, physician to the Greek gods, because the old European variety, *Paeonia officinalis*, was looked on as an elixir for all ills. It

### Handsome is...

*A fine group of waterside plants, all with good foliage: Rodgersia pinnata, bronze-leaved R. pinnata 'Superba', Astilboides tabularis with huge rounded, jagged leaves and the glaucous blue leaves of Hosta 'Big Daddy'.*

was said to cure jaundice, kidney pains and epilepsy, to prevent nightmares and lift depression. It took off as a garden flower in the mid-nineteenth century when the French nurserymen Calot, Dessert and Crousse began some fancy cross-breeding, using *P. officinalis* with the Chinese species *P. lactiflora*. There are now at least 150 hybrids to choose from, as well as some elegant species.

The common double crimson opens in late spring, most of the hybrids in early summer. Doubles last longer in flower than singles, but are more difficult to stake and keep the right way up if there is a rainstorm. There is a third type, sometimes called Imperials, sometimes anemone-flowered. They have strong, bowl-shaped outer petals like the singles, but the stamens have turned into thread-like petals, making a huge fluffy boss in the centre of each flower. Sometimes these are the same colour as the outside petals, sometimes they contrast. 'Bowl of Beauty' is a good peony of this type, rich pink petals with a creamy white centre. 'Globe of Light', is similar, pure rose with a rich gold centre. 'White Wings' is a fine single peony, white with foliage that, in the right soils, colours well in autumn. 'Sir Edward Elgar' is a bright single maroon, free-flowering and slightly later than 'White Wings'. Try peonies with a carpet of London pride (*Saxifraga* x *urbium*) in front, a cardoon (*Cynara cardunculus*) behind, a sprawl of blue *Geranium* x *magnificum* by the side or spikes of some piercing cobalt delphiniums.

*Paeonia lactiflora* 'Bowl of Beauty', p.92

Of the doubles, there is no end. 'Cornelia Shaylor' is a good one, with rose flowers almost 15cm (6in) across. 'Monsieur Jules Elie' is a medium-sized pink washed over with a lilac-grey, the petals curling in on themselves to make a fluffy ball. It is very free-flowering and grows about 90cm (36in) tall. Some varieties are more sweetly scented than others. 'Glory of Somerset', a clear heliotrope pink, is extra smelly. So is the elegant 'Madame Calot', with pale pink and creamy-white flowers. Henry Mitchell, gardening correspondent of the *Washington Post*, described the doubles as "dahlias that have gone to heaven". Use them with brunnera and the brilliant spurge *Euphorbia polychroma* to transform late spring borders.

*Euphorbia polychroma* 'Major', p.42

## THE ALLIUM BRIGADE

Alliums, together with anemones, camassias, muscari and galtonia all carry the bulb display from late spring through into summer. The alliums are an enormous family with more than 120 sorts listed by specialist growers. They are found wild all over the northern hemisphere, in the Middle East, western China, the Alps, the Mediterranean and the Pyrenees. Most are hardy and easy to grow. The outline of the flower, usually a firm, round ball balanced on top of a sturdy stem, is strong and well defined – useful among the amorphous mounds and hummocks of herbaceous border plants. *Allium cernuum* will give a good display for a month in early summer. It has wiry stems about 45cm (18in) long topped with drooping clusters of small, bead-like, pinkish-purple flowers, 20 or more in each head. It is an elegant sight and there is not too much of the undistinguished foliage to detract from the main event. Try it with the black-faced viola 'Molly Sanderson' and blue-grey *Alchemilla erythropoda*. Most alliums do best in well-drained soil in full sun. If you grow them among herbaceous plants, stick them well down in the earth, 12–15cm (5–6in) deep. This makes it more unlikely that you will spear them on your fork during the autumn clean-up when you may well have forgotten their existence.

Some alliums are as good in death as they are in life. This is especially true of *A. hollandicum*, *A. cristophii* and *A. schubertii* which, as they die, become huge greenish or buff drumsticks on stiff stems. *Allium cristophii* has a stout stem, only 60cm (24in) high, and stands up well to bad weather. The biggest heads are 20–25cm (8–10in) across, perfectly round and made up of masses of starry soft purple flowers. Each has six thin symmetrical petals and the flowers cluster in a ball at the top of the stem, a firework frozen at the moment of explosion. Try it with catmint and the tall white phlox 'Miss Lingard'. It also looks lovely rising from a hazy spread of sky blue nigella, or jostling the rich violet flowers of *Geranium* x *magnificum*. You could perhaps try one of the taller alliums interplanted with silybum, a plant like a variegated thistle that is rather better in youth than it is in old age, a cruel thing to say, but true. It is a biennial, dangerously domestic-looking in its first year, when it hugs the ground with crinkly foliage, the dark leaves splashed and veined with silver. In the second year comes an immense flowering stem. Then death. Time to try a different combination. With the smaller alliums, such as *A. caeruleum*, which has flowerheads no bigger than a golf ball, you need correspondingly small companions. Try it on a rockery or scree, between low-growing mounds of a variegated thyme, with thrift or among grey-foliaged pinks.

## IS VARIEGATION A GOOD THING?

Gardeners often suppose that any variegated plant will be a better choice than the plain-leaved alternative. Not so. It is true of silybum, which is only worth growing for its silver-splashed leaves. They look wonderful interspersed with the feathery foliage of young fennel plants. Nevertheless, too many variegated plants in the garden can look like a bad outbreak of spotty rash. And some variegated plants just look sickly, gasping for a good dose of chlorophyll. But carefully used, variegated plants are winners. First, as always, you should think about what the plant needs in order to grow successfully. Some need to be in shade if the leaves are to stay strongly marked. Others will do best in full sun. Second, bear in mind that in any mixed group, a variegated plant will be the one that draws the eye. It will do best in an unfussy setting, with plants that are strong enough not to be browbeaten by their showier neighbour.

The variegated comfrey *Symphytum* x *uplandicum* 'Variegatum' is a plant that always attracts attention. It is a coarse, brash, magnificent thing with great hairy leaves in two shades of grey-green, each with a wide margin of creamy white. The leaves emerge in mid-spring, and in late spring the plant throws up flower spikes of a blueish mauve which will stay looking good until early summer. When the leaves start to look dog-eared (and they will), you must shear the whole plant down to the ground. It will throw up a second crop of good leaves, which have a much longer season than the first.

But this splendid bully will completely terrorize feathery companions such as astilbe or achillea. If you think the comfrey's bold leaf will be a good anchor for them, you will be wrong. It will drown them. Try it instead in front of a stand of angelica which will give it a cool, but architectural, setting. The angelica will not be cowed, as other plants may be, by the comfrey's power play. It is powerful enough itself.

*Angelica gigas*, p.90

# *Too many variegated plants in the garden can look like a bad outbreak of spotty rash.*

In pulmonarias, variegation is a must. The plain-leaved ones are not half such good doers and contribute far less after the spring flowering period. Where you might want a plain green and blue effect, rather than using *Pulmonaria angustifolia* 'Munstead Blue', try omphalodes, which flowers much more freely and brightly. The variegated *Pulmonaria saccharata* is particularly pleasant, with pointed leaves splashed rather than spotted with silver. The flower spikes come through in early to mid-spring, with blooms that drift between pink and blue. Then there is a hearty crop of leaves, very useful under some fairly plain, tall planting, ferns perhaps – or giant fennel. In a white garden, 'Sissinghurst White' would be the one to go for.

*Pulmonaria* 'Lewis Palmer', p.158

*Ferula communis*, p.152
*Pulmonaria* 'Sissinghurst White', p.26

Astrantia is always a good-tempered plant, variegated or not, with flowers that have the curious papery texture of everlastings. *Astrantia major* 'Sunningdale Variegated' is particularly choice, with leaves splashed boldly with cream. It looks very good alongside the plain blue-flowered brunnera, or next to the purple-flushed leaves of the herbaceous clematis *C. recta* 'Purpurea'. A dark-leaved bugle (such as *Ajuga reptans* 'Atropurpurea'), running around its base, suits it too.

## THROW AWAY THE RULE BOOK

New gardeners desperately want rules to help them make sense of what they need to do in the garden. But the wonderful thing about gardening is that, each year, plants behave differently, as they respond to the conditions around them. One summer they might have to cope with a drought. Sometimes, but not always, they will be tripped up by a particularly prolonged bout of freezing weather. Rules aren't as important as principles. If you understand the principle of why, for instance, you shouldn't set out tender exotics or bedding plants too early in the year, then you know when you need to bend the general rules.

You need to understand the growth patterns of particular plants, too, in order to get the best out of them. Take the dark-leaved cow parsley *Anthriscus sylvestris* 'Ravenswing', a mighty takeable plant, if you see it early in the growing season when its foliage, dark and sumptuous, is at its best. But then, it collapses, like its wild relative, so it is no use including it in groups which peak in high summer. It is a creature of late spring and early summer only, marvellous with another cow-parsleyish thing, actually a type of chervil, *Chaerophyllum hirsutum* 'Roseum', with lilac-mauve flowers, or a fancy form of Jacob's ladder such as *Polemonium* 'Sonia's Bluebell', which has paler blue flowers and darker, more bronzed foliage than the species. Another good companion is sisyrinchium, which gives upright sword-shaped, iris-like leaves in places where irises wouldn't be happy. The prettiest of the tribe is a small cream-striped sisyrinchium called *S. striatum* 'Aunt May'. It bears pale creamy flowers on top of stiff, fan-like foliage, no more than 30cm (12in) high.

Gradually you begin to learn about connecting various events in a bed or border, joining up separate incidents, separate groups, to make a single flowing tapestry of plants. In this enterprise, you need to learn who your best friends are. They will be big, soft billowing plants like catmint, good enough to be stars themselves, but also capable of reaching out softly and joining hands with other plants around, plants that were not part of the original group you had set the catmint with.

## Close-knit community

*Bowles' golden grass,* Milium effusum *'Aureum', a fine form of the British native, is spectacular in late spring when its gamboge-yellow colour is most intense. Here it is partnered with the delicate locket flowers of* Dicentra formosa.

Catmint makes an excellent buffer plant because it makes soft mounds of growth and its texture is matt and gentle. The foliage is good from spring, when it first appears, right up to autumn, when it begins to look tired and worn, as well it might after six months on show. 'Six Hills Giant' is a richly generous catmint, but you need to give it room. It will grow 90cm (36in) up as well as out. Perhaps when you first planted that catmint, you were still in a swoony state about white gardens (though you will grow out of that, sooner or later – sooner is better). You bought a handsome white phlox, carefully choosing one of the *Phlox maculata* types rather than the more common *Phlox paniculata* because it does not get nibbled by eelworm.

The phlox does all that you had hoped, flowering in luxuriant columns, rather than terminal pyramids, but you begin to wonder whether the colour scheme, tasteful pale greyish blue and ultra-tasteful white, isn't, well, a bit limiting. And you have been reading a book about foliage in the garden. You have been told you need some important leaves somewhere in

*Gradually you begin to learn about connecting separate incidents, separate groups to make a single flowing tapestry of plants.*

what you are now thinking of as your composition. For leaves, read hostas. You fancy warming the scene up a bit (daring) and decide on a goldish sort of hosta rather than a white-variegated one. Because you are feeling impatient, you splash out on three hostas, perhaps 'Fragrant Gold' or 'Lemon Lime', and plant them by the phlox. The whole group swings instantly into a different mode. The warming happens. The balance shifts.

*Hosta* 'Lemon Lime', p.144

Then, having enjoyed these plants all the way through from late spring to autumn, you begin to worry about the yawning gap that is going to stretch from autumn round to the following late spring. The three plants you have so far brought together will take you through a long season, passing the baton from one to the other as the months move on, but they still leave you with nothing for early spring. Anemones are the answer, the fat-stemmed, chubby De Caen type. Planted in autumn, these will give you three months of spring flowers – white, pale blue, purple, pink and magenta. The foliage is bright green and ferny. Exuberance is what you need in spring and anemones have that in abundance. They are so free flowering that you can pick a fresh potful every week and still not see any gaps in the display. Now you are beginning to weave the blanket that will eventually stretch to cover all your garden with a shimmering, shifting pattern of flowers and leaves. The catmint and the phlox, the hostas and the anemones make a web, which will reach out to touch other webs that you will be creating in neighbouring patches of ground. Before you know it, you will have a joined-up garden. No gardener ever wants the months of late spring and early summer, with their eruptions, their affirmations of life, ever to finish. Making sure there is more still to come softens the blow. □

*Anemone coronaria* De Caen Group, p.32

# Aquilegia vulgaris 'Nora Barlow' *with* Crocus chrysanthus 'Ladykiller' *and* Dianthus 'Musgrave's Pink'

Aquilegias are such shameless cross-breeders, it is impossible to keep named varieties true to type. Self-seeding is to be encouraged though, as new types crop up each season. 'Nora Barlow' is particularly promiscuous, and produces a huge family of granny's bonnets, all different. These types, including the flat-faced clematis-flowered aquilegias, are much easier to keep in cultivation than the long-spurred types, but you need both. They all like heavy soil, are equally happy in sun or shade and have handsome greyish foliage, an asset even when the plant is not flowering. Do not be in too much of a hurry to cut down the stems after flowering. The plants can be tidied up in late summer, when they will produce fresh mounds of foliage of the same greyish hue as the dianthus. The crocus flowers will take care of early spring and the pinks (modern kinds at least) will flower, though sporadically, until early autumn.

**Aquilegia vulgaris 'Nora Barlow' (Columbine or granny's bonnet)**
**Height** *90cm (36in).*
**Spread** *45cm (18in).*
**Flowering time** *Late spring to early summer.*
**Star qualities** *Pink, green and cream flowers. Elegant foliage is a good foil for bulbs.*
**Other varieties** *'Melton Rapids' has inky-blue clematis-style flowers; 'Nivea' is pure white. Long-spurred McKana Hybrids are beautiful but more difficult to keep.*

**Crocus chrysanthus 'Ladykiller'**
*Tightly wrapped buds open in early spring to produce white goblets, heavily flushed on the outside with purple. The flowers are delicate, smaller and earlier than the fat Dutch crocus which follow. Where happy, in well-drained soil, Crocus chrysanthus will increase rapidly to make dense clumps. 'Blue Pearl' and 'Cream Beauty' are equally good varieties.*

**Dianthus 'Musgrave's Pink'**
*This pink is sometimes called 'Green Eyes' and you can see why, with its neat, acid-green centre. It is an elegant pink, though not as long in its flowering as other more modern varieties. 'Prudence' has double flowers of pale pink, laced with crimson round the margins. Clove-scented 'Alice' is equally good, as is the old-fashioned 'Dad's Favourite' (see p.150).*

*Aquilegia vulgaris 'Nora Barlow'* ▷

# Convallaria majalis *with* Helleborus argutifolius *and* Epimedium x perralchicum

Lily-of-the-valley (*Convallaria*) is an old favourite that grows from a branched, creeping, horizontal rhizome. It hates being disturbed and is slow to settle when first planted. Where it is suited, that is, where the soil is cool, rich and damp, it spreads rapidly. The fresh green leaves are quite strong enough to keep out weeds. The variety 'Fortin's Giant' has larger flowers than the ordinary lily-of-the-valley. It also has broader foliage and the useful tendency to flower a week or 10 days later than the plain species. Plant both to extend the season of flowering. To maintain vigour, top-dress the rhizomes with leaf-mould each autumn. Both the epimedium and the hellebore will enjoy the same cool, shady places in the garden as the lily-of-the-valley. The hellebore will be the first into flower, followed by the epimedium, and that will overlap with the lily-of-the-valley. The epimedium's evergreen leaves take on burnished tints in autumn, but in the main, this is a group for spring interest.

*Convallaria majalis*
(Lily-of-the-valley)
**Height** *30cm (12in).*
**Spread** *30cm (12in).*
**Flowering time** *Late spring.*
**Star qualities** *Swoony scent on flowers which last a long time when picked. Creeping rhizomes will colonize damp shady areas in the garden.*
**Other varieties** *'Albostriata' has leaves neatly pinstriped in creamy white; 'Flore Pleno' has double white flowers; C. majalis var. rosea has flowers of pale pinky mauve.*

### Helleborus argutifolius

*This species has perhaps the most handsome foliage of this extravagantly well-endowed group. The leaves are three-lobed, each of the stiff leaflets joined to the top of the stalk and edged all round with mock prickles. The green is matt and olive, a perfect foil for the great mounds of cup-shaped flowers that open in late winter. It grows equally happily in full sun or shade.*

### Epimedium x perralchicum
### (Barrenwort)

*The leaves of this ground-covering plant are rather more important than the flowers. This one is evergreen and they are there all year; the flowers are ephemeral. Epimediums include both evergreen and deciduous species. The foliage of all is good, but to get the best effect at flowering time, you should shear off the old leaves on deciduous types in late winter, and tidy up the evergreens, so that the blooms can be more easily seen.*

*Convallaria majalis* ▷

# Crambe cordifolia *with* Ranunculus ficaria 'Brazen Hussy' *and* Tropaeolum majus 'Jewel of Africa'

You can use crambe like a lighthouse to mark a promontory in the garden, or to fit into a curve in a path. It is not an easy plant to combine with others. In growth, it takes up an enormous amount of room and its huge, rhubarb leaves flatten anything within a metre of its crown. It demands space in all directions, upwards and out. But when the leaves melt away in late autumn, there is nothing but a knobby growing point, bare earth all around. This is why the celandine is such a help, for it comes out in winter, and will cover the ground around the crambe. Its own leaves will have packed themselves away long before the crambe gets into growing gear. For added summer interest, nasturtiums will haul themselves up the crambe's stout flowering stems. The crambe's own flowers will have finished long before the nasturtium has started. For safety, set the nasturtiums out as young plants, grown from seed in 7cm (3in) pots. They will die down with the first frosts, but the ghostly dried flowerheads of the crambe will stand through winter.

### Crambe cordifolia
**Height** *2.5m (8ft).*
**Spread** *1.5m (5ft).*
**Flowering time** *Late spring to midsummer.*
**Star qualities** *Huge, puckered, dark green leaves. Tall, strong stems bear wide, airy panicles of tiny white flowers. The skeleton flower stems stand until midwinter and look splendid rimed with frost.*
**Other varieties** *Crambe maritima hugs the ground, giving an entirely different effect. The foliage is better (more glaucous) but the plant does not have the architectural quality of its tall cousin.*

### Ranunculus ficaria 'Brazen Hussy' (Celandine)
*Many gardeners look on celandines as weeds, but this is a special weed, with leaves that are a deep chocolate brown, although still as glossy as the foliage of an ordinary celandine. The bright yellow flowers have a chocolate flush on the backs of the petals. Though the flowers are scarcely 5cm (2in) high, the celandine will quickly spread to make solid mats of foliage.*

### Tropaeolum majus 'Jewel of Africa' (Nasturtium)
*Grown from seed, this vigorous nasturtium will easily climb to 2.5m (8ft) in a season, the variegated leaves underpinning flowers in yellow, red, cream and apricot. If you want a calmer, less riotous effect, choose a variety such as 'Whirlybird Cream', which has plain green leaves and flowers like creamy buttermilk.*

# Dicentra 'Stuart Boothman' *with* Anemone nemorosa 'Robinsoniana' *and* Clematis recta 'Purpurea'

Purples and pinks ebb and flow through this group of plants, centred on the fine dicentra 'Stuart Boothman'. If you want to make the whole group larger, use one of the bigger dicentras, such as *D. spectabilis*, though you will lose the advantage of the grey foliage, which contrasts well with the purplish tones of the herbaceous clematis. In terms of flowers, the season will start with the dicentra and the wood anemones, which have the fragile, consumptive air of flowers that are not long for this earth. In the hurly-burly of summer, they would not be strong enough to hold their ground, but in spring, there is space for them to languish elegantly in the garden. The rhizomes look unpromising – shapeless pieces of fossilized Plasticine – but the transformation from toad to prince is astounding. The dicentra will probably flower longer than the anemones but not long enough to coincide with the clematis, which carries interest through to autumn with its fluffy seedheads.

**Dicentra 'Stuart Boothman'**
Height *30cm (12in).*
Spread *40cm (16in).*
Flowering time *Mid-spring to early summer.*
Star qualities *Beautiful grey, finely cut foliage. Pink flowers which hang like little lockets along the stems.*
Other varieties *'Langtrees' has grey foliage with white flowers. D. spectabilis has far showier flowering stems, but the foliage is green. D. spectabilis 'Alba' makes a big plant, up to 1.2m (4ft) high with showy white flowers dangling from the stems.*

**Anemone nemorosa 'Robinsoniana' (Wood anemone)**
*From this anemone come delicate, very pale blue-mauve windflowers, 12cm (5in) high, with darkish green, finely cut foliage. 'Alba Plena' is a double white form which is reasonably vigorous when happy. Wood anemones should not be planted too deep: 2.5cm (1in) of earth on top of the rhizomes is plenty. Moist, cool, shady, humus-rich soil is what they like best.*

**Clematis recta 'Purpurea'**
*Although this is a herbaceous clematis, not a climber, it does best with some support, when it will reach 2m (6ft). This form has good foliage, markedly purple when young, though becoming greenish as the plant ages. Choose carefully. Some forms are far better than others. From midsummer to autumn, the clematis is covered with a mass of tiny white flowers, heavily scented.*

*Dicentra* 'Stuart Boothman' ▷

# Dryopteris wallichiana *with* Aquilegia longissima *and* Ajuga reptans 'Atropurpurea'

Ferns, like spurges, are reliable "bankers", provided you can give them the cool conditions they like, and they make superb long-term companions for more ephemeral plants. For looks, you cannot do better than *Dryopteris wallichiana*, tall, elegant, formally and soberly suited but without a hint of stuffiness. The fronds, uncurling in late spring, arrange themselves with the easy poise that comes of 400 million years of breeding. "Is that it?" you might ask. "No flowers? No fruit? No smell?" No, none of those. This is the horticultural equivalent of the very plain, very expensive little black dress. *Dryopteris filix-mas* is common in the temperate zones of the northern hemisphere, but *D. wallichiana* comes from Central Asia and has a fairly dangerous air about it, unusual in ferns. It will sweep elegantly out of the mat of bugle round its feet and hold its own, even when the yellow-flowered aquilegia bursts into bloom in early summer.

### *Dryopteris wallichiana*

**Height** *90cm (36in)*.
**Spread** *75cm (30in)*.
**Star qualities** *Elegant shuttlecock shape. Midribs thickly covered with dark brown scales, which look like fur. The fronds, when they first emerge in spring, are brilliant yellowish green.*
**Other varieties** D. filix-mas, *the common male fern, is tougher but does not have the wonderful hairy midribs of* D. wallichiana.

### Aquilegia longissima

*This beautiful aquilegia grows wild on the prairies of southern Arizona and western Texas. Mounds of ferny foliage are topped by soft yellow, spurred flowers, delicately scented. It is not as long-lived in the garden as the common granny's bonnet but it is easy to raise from seed and, where happy, will self-seed. The flowering stems are at least 60cm (24in) high. Cut them down after the seed has been shed.*

### Ajuga reptans 'Atropurpurea' (Bugle)

*In the wild, bugle chooses cool, moist, shady places to grow and will do best in the same conditions in the garden. It is an effective colonizer, rooting overground as it goes, but should not be allowed to rampage among delicate neighbours. 'Atropurpurea' has highly polished bronze-purple foliage, topped in early summer with small spires of deep blue flowers no more than 10cm (4in) high.*

*Dryopteris wallichiana*

# Euphorbia characias *with* Eremurus x isabellinus 'Cleopatra' *and* Geranium pratense 'Plenum Violaceum'

The star here is the most splendid of all foliage plants, making a solid clump with many stems springing from the base. The stems have a biennial habit. For their first year, they make foliage. In the spring of their second year, some produce great domes of sulphurous yellow–green flowers (some cultivars better than others). Meanwhile new shoots are being produced from the base, so there is an ever-rolling supply of new growth and no off-season gap. Cold spring winds may burn the foliage so try to give this euphorbia a position out of the worst draughts. It will provide a good screen for the lower half of the eremurus, whose flowering spikes will tower above it. The eremurus's leaves choose to die at a bad moment, when the flowering spikes are at their best. If you plant your eremurus behind the spurge, you won't see its dying foliage. The double-flowered cranesbill (*Geranium*) will coincide with the last gasps of the spurge flowers and peak with the eremurus, whose stately spikes, covered in seedheads, can stand skeleton-like through early winter.

### Euphorbia characias
**Height** *1.2m (4ft).*
**Spread** *1.2m (4ft).*
**Flowering time** *Early spring to early summer.*
**Star qualities** *Landmark plant with superb, glaucous foliage, held in whorls round the stem. Evergreen. Big flowerheads of intense greenish yellow.*
**Other varieties** *Foliage in some types is bluer than others and some varieties have particularly showy flowers. 'John Tomlinson' has big, almost spherical flower heads, nearly 40cm (16in) long; 'Lambrook Gold' has cylindrical flowerheads, more golden in colour.*

### Eremurus x isabellinus 'Cleopatra' (Foxtail lily)
*The fleshy roots of this magnificent plant radiate out from the crown like the spokes of a wheel. They need to be planted carefully in well-drained ground. Lax clumps of strap-shaped leaves die away as the huge flowering stems are produced. The stems are thickly set with small star-shaped flowers, to make eye-catching columns. 'Cleopatra' is orange, but there are white, pink, yellow and apricot forms.*

### Geranium pratense 'Plenum Violaceum' (Cranesbill)
*Deeply divided leaves make a clump up to 60cm (24in) high and wide. In the right conditions, the foliage colours well in autumn. 'Plenum Violaceum' has double flowers of a wonderful deep violet-blue which come out in high summer and last for several weeks, longer than the single-flowered types. Arrange some twiggy sticks for the lax stems to scramble through.*

*Euphorbia
charracias*

# Gladiolus communis subsp. byzantinus *with*
# Limonium platyphyllum *and* Geranium palmatum

All these plants like light, free-draining soil in full sun. The gladiolus does not have as dominant a presence as the geranium and the sea lavender, which is why you should treat it as the star of the group. Although in light soils, it spreads reasonably well by seed and stolon, it is much slower to bulk up in heavy soils. Start off with a generous clutch of corms, otherwise it will be visually overpowered by the wide-reaching arms of the geranium and sea lavender. The geranium is particularly useful in early spring, when, if the winter has been mild, it is already spreading out its handsome leaves, each held on a single stiff stem, to make clumps 1.2m (4ft) across. In this early part of the year, before the gladiolus starts to flower, it makes an excellent foil for early tulips. Flowering in this group will be sequential: after the gladiolus will come huge heads of pink flowers on the geranium, followed by a late summer eruption from the sea lavender.

**Gladiolus communis subsp. *byzantinus***
Height *1m (3ft).*
Spread *8cm (3in).*
**Flowering time** *Late spring to early summer.*
**Star qualities** *Deep magenta flowers that, oddly, are not difficult to combine with other colours, especially pinks and blues. Sword-like foliage.*
**Other varieties** *This wild gladiolus is a world away from the top-heavy gladioli of the show bench. Avoid them in mixed plantings. White-flowered 'The Bride' is beautiful, but not hardy.*

### Limonium platyphyllum (Sea lavender)
*The dark green leathery leaves make an evergreen rosette from which, in late summer, spring tall wiry stems of flower. They branch widely, making clouds of lavender-blue, and the flowers last a long time in the garden. Stems can also be cut and dried to make "everlastings" for flower arrangements. 'Blue Cloud' is a good selected form, with stems reaching 60cm (24in).*

### Geranium palmatum
*This geranium comes from Madeira, so is not reliably hardy, though it is a shade tougher than its close cousin G. maderense. In summer, both have tall showy panicles of pink flowers (not a good pink unfortunately) which stand at least a metre (3ft) high, but the point of these plants is their foliage. It is glossy, beautifully shaped and, where the weather is not too vile, evergreen. It self-seeds, but you need to transplant the seedlings early. The plants have long tap roots to sustain them in Madeiran droughts and they resent being mauled about.*

*Gladiolus communis*
subsp. *byzantinus*

# Iris 'Jane Phillips' *with* Crocus speciosus *and* Tulipa orphanidea Whittallii Group

The name, iris, comes from the Greek word meaning rainbow and the colours of the flowers make a reasonable job of covering the spectrum. Only a true red is missing and the family is strongest on the blue, indigo, violet end of the scale. The reddish ones are actually tawny brown. The kind of place bearded irises grow best is a narrow border, such as might run alongside a pergola or a path, where they can be in full sun but not have to share their space with too many other plants. Big bearded irises, such as 'Jane Phillips', are not generally good mixers as they need the sun on their rhizomes to bake them. A sprinkling of some light-limbed annual, such as love-in-a-mist (*Nigella*), would work, but the ideal companions are bulbs, which, performing at different seasons, then put themselves neatly away until they are next wanted. Bearded irises' own flowering season is early summer, so to spread the flowering time, use autumn-flowering bulbs as well as spring-flowering ones.

*Iris* 'Jane Phillips'
**Height** *100cm (39in).*
**Spread** *60cm (24in).*
**Flowering time** *Late spring to early summer.*
**Star qualities** *Gorgeous sky-blue flowers on long stems. Sword foliage gives interest before the flowers appear.*
**Other varieties** *Tall bearded irises are the most stately, but there are medium and short hybrids, too. 'Arctic Fancy' (intermediate) is white with violet markings; 'Bibury' (dwarf) is white with pale yellow hafts; 'Bromyard' (dwarf) has greyish petals overlaid with gold.*

## Crocus speciosus

*We think of crocus as spring-flowering bulbs, but this one performs in autumn. The solitary flowers, up to 5cm (2in) long, appear before the leaves. The species is violet-blue, but there is a variety, 'Albus', that is pure white. 'Conqueror' has deep blue flowers. All will spread rapidly by seed and offsets.*

## Tulipa orphanidea Whittallii Group

*Here you have an outstanding tulip, no more than 30cm (12in) high, with neat, pointed petals. The colour is a burnt orange caramel, very distinct and unusual. The outer petals are smaller than the inner ones and are flushed with a pale creamy buff on the reverse. The flower makes a perfect rounded bud with all the petals meeting at a sharp point in the middle. There is a smoky, indeterminate basal blotch, greenish black with a yellow halo, the dark colour drifting slightly up the veins of the petals, like watercolour paint on wet paper.*

*Iris* 'Jane Phillips' ▷

# Iris sibirica *with* Fritillaria imperialis *and* Lilium 'Black Dragon'

This trio has little but flower power to offer the gardener. But what flowers! From time to time, you need to abandon precepts about foliage and texture and form of plants and succumb to pure hedonism. The iris will probably overlap with the crown imperial, so keep in mind a clear idea of the colours you want to combine. The crown imperial offers a limited range – foxy brownish-orange to clear yellow – but the Siberian irises are available in a wide range of blues, mauves, whites and yellows. Remember that the bright yellow of the crown imperial will kill the much softer yellow of the irises. Dark-flowered 'Shirley Pope' would provide a splendid contrast. The iris's sheaves of leaves will act as a buffer and support for the lilies which can soar up behind these clumps of foliage. Neither iris nor fritillary smell good (the fritillary has a positively unpleasant, acrid smell), so be sure to choose a lily heavy with scent to see you through the summer. When the lily is over, there will be nothing until the formidable snout of the fritillary starts pushing through the ground again the following spring.

### Iris sibirica
**Height** *90cm (36in).*
**Spread** *60cm (24in).*
**Flowering time** *Mid- to late spring.*
**Star qualities** *Tough, hardy, easy to grow. Elegant, beardless flowers, like heraldic fleur-de-lys.*
**Other varieties** *There are more than a hundred varieties of* I. sibirica. *'Cambridge' is a good straight blue, splashed with clear yellow; 'Dreaming Yellow' has white standards and slightly ruffled, creamy-yellow falls; 'Flight of Butterflies' is rich blue with white veining on the falls.*

### Fritillaria imperialis (Crown imperial)
*Known in gardens since the sixteenth century, these magnificent fritillaries send up flowering stems in early spring, which shoot rapidly to 1–1.2m (3–4ft). Round the top is a ring of yellow bell flowers, surmounted by a pineapple tuft of leaves. There is an orange-red form called 'Rubra Maxima'. These are firework plants, short-lived but spectacular.*

### Lilium 'Black Dragon'
*A trumpet-shaped lily, up to 2m (6ft) high, with big white flowers, washed over on the backs of the petals with a dark, purplish red. The flowers face boldly outwards, all the better for sniffing, for this is a richly scented lily. The oriental hybrid 'Casa Blanca' also smells wonderful, but it is not so easy to grow.*

*Iris sibirica*

# Nectaroscordum siculum *with* Corydalis flexuosa 'China Blue' *and* Deschampsia cespitosa 'Goldtau'

This is a group in the modern style, not exactly minimal, but cool, restrained, the colours offbeat. It features a particularly elegant grass; grasses have come a long way since grass meant lawn. Modern designers love them for their architectural forms and their seedheads, which persist long into winter. The nectaroscordum is angular and strange enough to be a designer darling too. Once, it was part of the big family of alliums. Now it has shifted sideways into a group of its own, containing little except itself, very exclusive. The most daring gasp of colour will come from the beautiful corydalis, pouring out a succession of lippy, tubular flowers from late spring. It will probably overlap with the nectaroscordum's flowers. But this is a plant that looks as good in seed as it does in flower. The seedheads form little caskets, multi-faceted, and they turn to face upwards, where the flowers had faced down. The tufted hair grass, like all grasses, has a long season of interest and its summer flowering heads will provide a fine contrast with the nectaroscordum's seedheads.

### Nectaroscordum siculum

**Height** *1.2m (4ft).*
**Spread** *10cm (4in).*
**Flowering time** *Early to midsummer.*
**Star qualities** *Tall, stiff stems bear heads of bell-shaped flowers, hanging bashfully downwards. These are a strange colour, not quite pink, not quite green or grey.*
**Other varieties** N. *subsp.* bulgaricum *is very similar, but there is more purple than pink in the flowerheads. A tall allium, such as* A. hollandicum, *could be used instead.*

### Corydalis flexuosa 'China Blue'

*From late spring to summer, this corydalis produces dense spikes of brilliant blue flowers, above bright green, ferny foliage. It prefers rich, moist but well-drained soil in partial shade but rarely makes a clump more than 20cm (8in) across. Group several plants for maximum impact. 'Purple Leaf' as its name suggests, is a form with bronze-purple foliage, a beautiful echo of the nectaroscordum's flowers.*

### Deschampsia cespitosa 'Goldtau' (Tufted hair grass)

*The species is one of the biggest and most beautiful of the grasses native to Britain and much of Europe. In the wild, it favours damp, acid soil, producing dense tussocks of narrow dark leaves and tall, strong flowering stems up to 1.2m (4ft). 'Goldtau' makes elegant plumes of tiny purplish-green flowers. By autumn, the spikes have faded to pale creamy yellow.*

*Nectaroscordum*
*siculum*

# Osmunda regalis *with* Angelica gigas *and* Rodgersia pinnata 'Superba'

You can use the royal fern, *Osmunda regalis*, to great effect in a garden, provided the soil is damp. It does not mind sun as long as its roots are moist and cool, but remember that it takes a little while to build up to its full regal stature – 2m (6ft) at maturity. The ordinary kind of royal fern is grand, leafy, the green fronds turning clear butter yellow in autumn before they die down. In the wild, these are plants of the water margin – ditches in western Ireland are full of them – and they will not thrive without this gentle dampness around them at all times. They prefer acid soils to alkaline ones, but this is not such an important requirement as wetness. Use royal ferns with plants that like the same conditions; they are natural companions for rodgersias of all kinds, and you could also try them with tall yellow flag irises or round-leaved ligularias. Here fern and rodgersia are teamed with a handsome purple-flowered angelica.

### Osmunda regalis (Royal fern)
**Height** *2m (6ft)*.
**Spread** *2m (6ft)*.
**Star qualities** *Beautiful bright green fronds uncurl in late spring to produce clumps of foliage about 1m (3ft) high. In summer, tall stems bearing clusters of rusty-brown spores appear between the leaves.*
**Other varieties** *'Cristata' has leaves with crested tips; 'Purpurascens' has foliage flushed in its early stage with bronze-purple.*

### Angelica gigas
*Biennial, like the common angelica, but A. gigas is blessed with stems and flowering heads of moody purple, rather than pale green. The flowering only happens in the second year. For the first year, the plant concentrates on building huge mounds of foliage, showy but smothering. Where suited, in damp, heavy soil, the flowering stems can reach 2m (6ft), but the flowers come later (late summer) than the ordinary angelica.*

### Rodgersia pinnata 'Superba'
*A splendid foliage plant with leaves like great hands, at least 30cm (12in) across, borne on strong stems. The flowers come late in the season and are carried well above the foliage, fluffy spikes of brilliant pink, rather like an astilbe's. 'Superba' gets its name because the leaves are particularly well burnished, like old leather.*

*Osmunda regalis*

# Paeonia lactiflora 'Bowl of Beauty' *with* Euphorbia schillingii *and* Lilium martagon var. album

There are three things you need to know if you are to succeed with peonies. Sadly for the peonies, many people know only two. Most important is the fact that they must not be planted too deep. On heavy soils, 2.5cm (1in) of earth on top of the crown is plenty. Even in light soils, twice that depth will be more than enough. Leaves may fight their way through, but if the plant is lodged suffocatingly deep, it will never flower. Secondly, peonies appreciate good food, plenty of humus and well-rotted manure dug into the ground during the summer before planting and a liberal measure of bone meal and mulch thereafter. The third rule has to do with the peony's temperament. It is an odd mixture of flash-in-the-pan and stayer. The flowers are dramatic, gaudy and short-lived, but the plant itself, once settled, lives an astonishingly long time. Although a peony may survive half a century of neglect, it cannot stand disturbance. If you move into a garden where a clump of peonies is well established and flowering, leave it alone. Just give it some good neighbours: here a fine spurge (*Euphorbia*) and some aristocratic white martagon lilies.

### Paeonia lactiflora 'Bowl of Beauty'

**Height** *80–100cm (32–39in).*
**Spread** *80–100cm (32–39in).*
**Flowering time** *Early summer.*
**Star qualities** *Very large deep pink petals make a shallow cup surrounding a fluffy centre of narrow, cream petaloids (stamens that look like petals). The early foliage provides a handsome foil for spring bulbs.*
**Other varieties** *'Laura Dessert' is a pale, creamy yellow, flushed with pink; 'Duchesse de Nemours' has large, fragrant, double white flowers; 'Félix Crousse' has big crimson-pink flowers, double, with ruffled petals.*

### Lilium martagon var. album

*Martagon lilies will grow in almost any well-drained soil in full sun or partial shade. The white form is exquisite: bright green stems up to 1.2m (4ft) with up to 50 small, nodding turkscap flowers hanging from each. They are very small – no more than 4cm (1½in) across – but the mass makes up for the individual.*

### Euphorbia schillingii

*The plantsman Tony Schilling introduced this plant not much more than 20 years ago from Nepal, and it quickly rose through the spurge ranks to become one of the five best. It grows up to 1m (3ft) making a clump of stems clothed in dark green leaves. In midsummer, these branch at the top to produce typical spurge flowerheads of greenish yellow, which last until mid-autumn. It is deciduous.*

*Paeonia lactiflora*
'Bowl of Beauty'

# Papaver orientale 'Patty's Plum' *with* Iris orientalis *and* Petunia 'Purple Wave'

Some gardeners are prejudiced against oriental poppies (and peonies) on the grounds that the flowers are short-lived. It is true, but they are so gorgeous, only a masochist would wish to be without them. When the poppy's short season is over, you can shear its coarse foliage down to the ground and use your petunias to cover the space instead. Being annuals, raised from seed, they cannot, anyway, go out into the garden until all danger of frost has passed. If you pot on your petunias into separate pots, where they can continue to grow happily, you need not set them out until the poppy has been cut down. By then they will be good, big plants and will come into flower quickly. In the meantime, while this scene-shifting has been going on, the stately iris will be holding the show together, flowering at the same time as the poppy, but staying on to help afterwards too. Its foliage is a great asset: it never needs staking, it seems immune to disease and it provides a fine foil to both poppy and petunia.

### Papaver orientale 'Patty's Plum'
**Height** *45–90cm (18–36in).*
**Spread** *60–90cm (24–36in).*
**Flowering time** *Late spring to midsummer.*
**Star qualities** *Extraordinary colour, a mixture of dove grey and washed-out purple.*
**Other varieties** *'Beauty of Livermere' has enormous flowers up to 20cm (8in) across of brilliant scarlet; 'Black and White' has white flowers with a dark crimson stain at the base of each petal; 'Cedric Morris' has soft pink flowers with frilled petals.*

### Iris orientalis

*New foliage is already well above ground in midwinter and eventually grows to as much as 1.2m (4ft). As a foliage plant alone, this iris earns its keep, for the sword leaves act as important punctuation marks among lower mounds of foliage and grow quickly to make large clumps. The fleur-de-lys flowers are white with yellow throats.*

### Petunia 'Purple Wave'

*The Wave series of F1 hybrid petunias produce extraordinarily vigorous plants, spreading at least a metre (3ft). Bred with hanging baskets and tubs in mind, they are equally good on the ground and flower abundantly over a long period until cold weather and frosty nights bring the show to an abrupt end. Single colours give a better effect than mixed.*

*Papaver orientale 'Patty's Plum'* ▷

# Polystichum setiferum 'Pulcherrimum Bevis' *with*
# Euphorbia x martinii *and* Galanthus 'Atkinsii'

Provided its roots stay moist and cool, this beautiful variant of the soft shield fern will grow quite happily in full sun, but it is perhaps seen to best advantage under trees, where it spreads out to make a swirling Catherine wheel of foliage. Each perfectly constructed green frond is supported by a pale brown midrib. Because it is an evergreen, you can set any number of more transitory partners alongside it, each of which it will effortlessly outclass. Flowers may come and go, but ferns such as 'Bevis' (discovered by an agricultural labourer of the same name along a Devon hedge-bank) go on forever. This is a long-lasting group of plants, with both the fern and the spurge (*Euphorbia*) providing a 12-month season of interest. The combination peaks in spring with the flowering of the snowdrop and the spurge, but long after they have gone, you will find yourself seeking out the fern to pay it rightful homage.

### *Polystichum setiferum* 'Pulcherrimum Bevis'
**Height** *60–80cm (24–32in).*
**Spread** *60–80cm (24–32in).*
**Star qualities** *Beautifully balanced, shuttlecock form. Fronds of exceptional elegance and texture.*
**Other varieties** *Ferns of the P. setiferum Plumosodivisilobum Group make more congested clumps, the fronds growing horizontally rather than vertically and often overlapping each other.*

### *Euphorbia x martinii*
*A native of the south of France, this spurge is technically a subshrub, rather than a perennial. Its upright stems make clumps of evergreen foliage up to 1m (3ft) high, the leaves tinged with a purplish red. Yellowish-green flowers with bright red centres are borne at the ends of the stems from mid-spring to midsummer.*

### *Galanthus 'Atkinsii'*
*Snowdrop fanciers spend most of late winter and early spring on their knees arguing about the provenance of their pet flowers. The main thing we ordinary mortals notice about 'Atkinsii' is that it is big, growing up to 20cm (8in), twice as high as the common snowdrop, G. nivalis. There is a heart-shaped green mark at the tip of each inner petal.*

*Polystichum setiferum* 'Pulcherrimum Bevis' ▷

# Pulsatilla vulgaris *with* Primula Cowichan Blue Group *and* Muscari comosum 'Plumosum'

If you use the suggested varieties, this group will glow with the brilliant colours of a jewel box: amethyst and sapphire. But there is plenty of room for manoeuvre. If you used a reddish-coloured Pasque flower (*Pulsatilla*) as a centrepiece, you could team it with one of the dark maroon-brown cowichans, and get quite a different effect. The grape hyacinth (*Muscari*) is gentle enough in colour to sit well with either combination. In essence, of course, this is a spring group, though the cowichans may start flowering in winter, if it is a mild one. By late spring, all the flowers may be out together, but after that there will be nothing to admire, except the Pasque flower's fluffy seedheads. These are all short plants. Use them to make a small group at the front of a border, or set them in adjacent pockets of a rockery.

### *Pulsatilla vulgaris* (Pasque flower)

**Height** *10–20cm (4–8in).*
**Spread** *20cm (8in).*
**Flowering time** *Mid- to late spring.*
**Star qualities** *Bell-shaped flowers in various shades of purple, covered with silky hairs. Long-lasting fluffy seedheads. Fern-like foliage, deeply cut.*
**Other varieties** *'Alba' has pure white flowers; 'Röde Klokke' has deep red flowers; 'Flore Pleno' is a double form; 'Barton's Pink' is a purplish magenta.*

### *Primula Cowichan Blue Group*

*There are many different primroses that you could use to partner the Pasque flower, but the cowichans are particularly striking: plain, self-coloured flowers, each with a tiny yellow eye. It is usually more effective in a garden to plant drifts of one colour, rather than mixtures. The cowichans produce flowers in dark reds, maroons and yellows. This is a clear blue, as blue as a primrose gets.*

### *Muscari comosum* 'Plumosum' (Grape hyacinth)

*This is a completely mad grape hyacinth that, at the moment of flowering, forgets what it set out to do. Instead of producing the tight little bells we are used to, it erupts into a fluff of tiny purplish thread, disarming and appealing. The leaves are no more than 15cm (6in) high but the flowers top them by a good 5cm (2in).*

*Pulsatilla vulgaris*

# Smyrnium perfoliatum *with* Tulipa 'Spring Green' *and* Myosotis sylvatica 'Music'

Smyrnium is not as often seen in gardens as you would expect, given its strange and memorable charm. It is wild at heart and has decided views on where it wants to be. Some gardeners find that scattering very fresh seed direct on the ground is the only way to get it to grow. Others say, emphatically, that you must start with good plants, set in moist, but well-drained soil. It is biennial, so the flowers come in the second year. After flowering, you have to depend on the plant's own self-seeding mechanism for a fresh supply of plants. In the wild, forget-me-nots (*Myosotis*) enjoy the same sort of conditions as the smyrnium, so they make natural companions (*see p. 45*). The exotic element is the tulip, which will float above the sea of forget-me-nots, poised and perfect. But the forget-me-nots must be tall and rangy enough to spread themselves through the tulip stems. Congested types will not work here. All three will flower together, though the smyrnium's flowers will outlive the other two.

**Smyrnium perfoliatum**
**Height** *60–120cm (2–5ft).*
**Spread** *60cm (24in).*
**Flowering time** *Late spring to early summer.*
**Star qualities** *Perfoliate leaves clasp the stem in an engaging way. Light, airy flowerheads have the same luminous green-yellow quality as a spurge's.*
**Other varieties** Smyrnium olusatrum, *commonly called Alexanders, has larger, more rounded flowerheads, but of a much less arresting colour.*

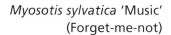

### Tulipa 'Spring Green'

*Like other Viridiflora tulips, 'Spring Green' has a broad green flame up the centre of each petal, the flame showing both on the back and the front. Extremely cool and elegant, the green flames are set against a ground of creamy white. Each petal has a slight sideways twist on it. The anthers are pale green, too.*

### Myosotis sylvatica 'Music' (Forget-me-not)

*Seed breeders seem determined to turn forget-me-nots into dwarfs, but for this grouping, avoid any types with 'Ball' or 'Mini' in their name and choose instead a cultivar such as 'Music' which, like the wild forget-me-not, reaches 24cm (10in) tall. We generally use these flowers as annuals, but they self-seed profusely, and make themselves as permanent as any perennial.*

*Smyrnium perfoliatum*

# Thalictrum aquilegiifolium *with* Phormium tenax Purpureum Group *and* Papaver somniferum 'Paeony Flowered'

**M**oody greys and purples dominate this group, which has little green about it at all. Both the thalictrum and the opium poppy (*Papaver somniferum*) have glaucous foliage, the waxy, washed-out effect strongest in the mounds of foliage that the poppies make before they shoot up to flower. All thalictrums are to be welcomed in the garden, though they will be happiest in areas where the summers are cool and damp. They prefer part shade to blazing sun. Most poppies like the opposite conditions, but *P. somniferum* will grow almost anywhere. After that, plants will perpetuate themselves by self-seeding. *Thalictrum aquilegiifolium* will start flowering just before the poppies come out. If you want collision rather than continuity, plant a later-flowering purple thalictrum (*see Other varieties, right*) instead. The phormium is the sheet anchor of the group, present, and looking much the same, for 12 months of the year.

### *Thalictrum aquilegiifolium*
**Height** *1m (3ft).*
**Spread** *45cm (18in).*
**Flowering time** *Early summer.*
**Star qualities** *Makes important clumps of finely cut, greyish-green foliage. Fluffy heads of purple flowers.*
**Other varieties** *'Thundercloud' has flowers of particularly intense purple;* T. delavayi *flowers later, from midsummer, with lilac flowers; its variety 'Hewitt's Double' has more richly coloured, longer-lasting flowers.*

### **Phormium tenax** Purpureum Group (New Zealand flax)
*Huge sword leaves stand stiffly up to 2m (6ft) or more. In this variety, the normal greyish green of the leaf is overlaid with a reddish purple. When well established, clumps send up vast plum-coloured flowering stems, bearing dull red flowers. The resulting seedheads look splendid in winter. The flax is not reliably hardy, but does particularly well in coastal areas.*

### *Papaver somniferum* 'Paeony Flowered' (Opium poppy)
*One of the most generous of annual flowers, with splendid glaucous foliage, beautiful flowers – in this variety up to 10cm (4in) across – and dramatic pepperpot seedheads. If you can find a selected seed strain of the double pink variety, buy it, or gradually select your own single-coloured strains from this bran-tub mixture.*

*Thalictrum aquilegiifolium* ▷

# Tulipa sprengeri *with* Viola riviniana Purpurea Group *and* Hosta 'Halcyon'

You have to make the most of *Tulipa sprengeri*, which opens from an oval bud to a starry flower with narrow pointed petals, because it is the last tulip you will see until the following spring. The colour is clear rather than brilliant, the backs of the outer petals washed over with buff suffused with olive and green. It increases from seed quite readily, sometimes flourishing in surprisingly shady positions under shrubs. Because tulips put themselves so completely away when they have finished flowering, they need some substantial companions. The viola, with its purplish foliage will normally be a permanent fixture and the hosta, whose greyish foliage works well with the purple viola, also has a long season, from mid-spring to mid-autumn. Add colchicums if you feel the two foliage plants need an extra autumn lift.

### Tulipa sprengeri
**Height** *50cm (20in).*
**Spread** *7cm (3in).*
**Flowering time** *Late spring to early summer.*
**Star qualities** *Clear red flower standing bolt upright on its stem.*
**Other varieties** *Other good earlier-flowering reds are 'Abba', a Double Early flowering in mid-spring, and 'Apeldoorn' and 'Gordon Cooper', Darwin Hybrids flowering in mid-spring.*

### Viola riviniana Purpurea Group
*This is the little violet until recently known as Viola labradorica 'Purpurea'. It is almost evergreen, or rather ever-purple, for its leaves are dark purplish green, an excellent foil for the pale violet-blue flowers that appear in late spring and early summer. It can be invasive, but is not difficult to control.*

### Hosta 'Halcyon'
*The leaves are bright grey-blue and at 20cm (8in) long, not too beefy. 'Halcyon' is one of the neat Tardiana Group of hostas and bears dense stems of flowers in summer, about 45cm (18in) tall. They, too, are lavender-grey, so the whole effect is very muted. The leaves collapse with the first frost, but return early the following spring.*

*Tulipa sprengeri*

# Viola 'Ardross Gem' *with* Crocus tommasinianus 'Barr's Purple' *and* Polemonium foliosissimum

Like many of life's enduring pleasures, violas do not grab you instantly by the throat. Operating little more than 15cm (6in) off the ground, they are not, anyway, built to be grabbers. They quietly creep up on you, enmeshing you without you realizing what is going on. At this moment in the gardening year, it is possible that nothing in your garden will give you more pleasure than mats of different violas. The flowers sit like well-drilled miniature rent-a-crowds, all gazing in the same direction, each bloom well-mannered enough not to get in the way of the one behind. They might be watching the Queen go by, a few rubber-neckers on each plant craning round the edge of the group to get a better view. It would have to be the Queen. Violas, being old-fashioned things, would never bother to line up for a flash in the pan like Madonna. Or even Hugh Grant. Though small, they are tenacious. All you have to do is deadhead them occasionally, a job to fit in as you wander round your garden in the evening, a glass of wine in hand. The crocus will extend the flowering season of this group back into early spring. The polemonium will partner the viola.

### Viola 'Ardross Gem'
**Height** *15cm (6in).*
**Spread** *30cm (12in).*
**Flowering time** *Late spring to late summer.*
**Star qualities** *Wonderful colour, rich mauve-blue, splashed with yellow on the chin. The blue is clearer and brighter than that of most violas.*
**Other varieties** *'Nellie Britton' (syn. 'Haslemere') is a dirty pink-mauve; 'Maggie Mott' is silvery mauve; 'Molly Sanderson' has black petals with the sheen of dangerously expensive satin.*

### Crocus tommasinianus 'Barr's Purple'
*The narrow furled buds of Crocus tommasinianus open out flat in the sun to show off their brilliant orange stigmas. 'Barr's Purple', like the similar 'Whitewell Purple', is a richer, deeper colour than the standard species. It is often flowering by late winter, clumps up rapidly and is altogether a paragon.*

### Polemonium foliosissimum
*The flowers come in the first half of summer, a long succession of lilac-coloured cups, but the foliage stays longer. Bright, juicy, vivid, the ferny leaves are made up of small leaflets neatly paired along the stem. Another species, P. caeruleum (Jacob's ladder), has bright blue flowers. Both grow to about 60cm (24in).*

# Zantedeschia aethiopica 'Crowborough'

## *with* Iris pseudacorus *and* Ligularia przewalskii

Damp, boggy soil at the edge of a pool will suit this trio best, though these plants are capable of growing away from water in any soil that is heavy and not too dry. The arum lily (*Zantedeschia*) is borderline hardy, but 'Crowborough', discovered in a Sussex garden, is hardier than most cultivars and more tolerant of dry soils. This is a group that needs space, for all three plants are bold, attention-seeking drama queens. They all have superb foliage, so even when the arum's fabulous white spathes, each guarding a yellow poker spadix, have finished, the vast, glossy leaves will continue to please. All three hold themselves beautifully, the deeply cut leaves of the ligularia contrasting with the smooth-edged arrows of the arum. Between them and around them, you can set the tall sword leaves of the iris, a foil for both the other plants. You scarcely need flowers with leaves as good as these, but the iris's yellow flags should coincide with the ligularia, both following on from the arum.

**Zantedeschia aethiopica 'Crowborough' (Arum lily)**

**Height** *90cm (36in).*
**Spread** *60cm (24in).*
**Flowering time** *Late spring to midsummer.*
**Star qualities** *Dramatic white spathes, waxy in texture. Handsome arrow-shaped foliage.*
**Other varieties** *'Green Goddess' has spathes tippped and tinged with green; 'Apple Court Babe' is much shorter than the norm, only 60cm (24in).*

### Iris pseudacorus (Yellow flag iris)

*A vigorous iris, with pale green leaves at least 90cm (36in) long. It enjoys damp soil, and in the wild grows at the margins of ponds and streams. The yellow flowers appear in midsummer, several to a stem, and come out in succession. There is a handsome variegated form, 'Variegata', with cream-striped foliage.*

### Ligularia przewalskii

*Excellent foliage, deeply cut, dark green and held on stems that are nearly black. The flowering stems, also black, rise up above the mounds of foliage to make tall yellow spires, which last from mid- to late summer. The stems will easily reach 2m (6ft) and the clumps spread boldly on damp soil to make important landmarks in a garden.*

A GARDEN IN HIGH SUMMER should be swimming with flowers and scent, for it is the peak of the gardening year. In uncertain spring and frost-prone autumn, we have to depend on hardy perennials that can withstand sudden plunges in temperature. In summer, we can spread sheets of annual flowers in the garden, to grow,

# high summer

flower and set seed within one breathless season. We can bring succulents and other tender plants out from the greenhouse to take their place in the summer parade. We can bed out temporary exotics among tougher and more permanent plants, where they sit, slightly sniffy, like film stars working in locations much less glamorous than they are themselves. These temporary plantings shift a garden into a different, more colourful gear. It is the garden's

### Colour takes the stage

*High summer explodes with a tumble of flowers in brilliant primary colours. Ruffed heads of* Eryngium x oliverianum *provide a buffer between the hot magenta tones of* Lychnis coronaria *and the yellow daisy flowers of* Coreopsis verticillata *behind.*

### Enter the reds

*One of the earliest crocosmias to flower, 'Lucifer' is also one of the best, throwing up tall stems of vivid red flowers. The foliage is excellent too: bright, clean and pleated down the whole of its length. The leaves make useful landmarks between lower mounds of perennials.*

equivalent of beachwear. Some ultra-sensitive gardeners shudder at the notion of bedding out. But there is nothing wrong with the flowers themselves – predominantly annuals and tender plants such as geraniums and salvias. The problem is the hackneyed way they are generally used. Salvias in bright red tunics are drilled in neat parallel rows, geraniums stand to attention in four-square formation, lobelia stands guard in front. There is absolutely no reason why bedding out should not escape the parade ground and join the aesthetes instead.

Bedding out is a mode of gardening very well suited to small town gardens. Small front urban patches need to sing hard for their supper and bedding out gives you the opportunity to try two (could be three) entirely different schemes in the same year. Most bedding schemes have too many

colours in them. Three is plenty. Two is better. Often you may find the happiest schemes come from using different shades of just one colour: soft yellows which encompass butter and cream, or a mixture of pale mauve and deep purple.

You can also give bedding schemes extra height and substance by using tall standards – it might be helichrysum, it might be a canna – among the ground-hugging plants that create the main carpet. There has to be a certain formality in the way they are placed. A circular bed calls for height at the centre. An oval bed could take either one or three tall standards. Most garden centres offer rather a limited range of bedding plants, often in mixed colours. To get the most subtle effects from annual bedding schemes, you will probably have to raise your own plants from seed.

Try, for instance, petunias with *Senecio cineraria*, which with very little effort creates an easy and effective blue and grey scheme. Sow petunia seed in early spring, using a weather-resistant plain blue variety such as 'Dreams Midnight Blue'. It should germinate in two weeks at a temperature of about 21°C (70°F). Prick out the seedlings, grow them on and harden them off before planting out in early summer. *Senecio cineraria* is not hard to find (but is often found under its old name, *Cineraria maritima*), either a filigree-leaved type such as 'Silver Dust' or a round-leaved variety like 'Cirrus'.

For a scheme in cream, grey and purple, start with several plants of variegated *Felicia amelloides*. The small, spoon-shaped leaves are variegated in cream and pale green and the daisy flowers are bright blue with yellow centres. They are good spreaders, but not hardy. Lift plants into pots for overwintering, or take softwood cuttings about 5cm (2in) long in mid- to late summer, to perpetuate your stock.

With the felicias use a dark-leaved heliotrope such as 'Chatsworth' or 'Marine'. The best types have leaves that are almost black, a sumptuous, rich background for the purple flowers. They last (in top condition) right through to late autumn, if there are no frosts to stop them in their tracks. The smell is heavenly, drifts of vanilla essence, tickled into action by the warmth of the sun. If you grow these plants from seed, remember to pinch out the tops when the seedlings are about 7cm (3in) high. This makes them bush out into serious space fillers.

Use standards of *Artemisia arborescens* to give height to this scheme. Buy plants with a strong main stem and train this up a bamboo cane, pinching out side-growths until you have a lollipop of growth on a stem 60–90cm (24–36in) high. If you want to gild the lily, add edgings of a marguerite (*Argyranthemum foeniculaceum*) with silver-grey leaves and white daisy flowers. 'Chelsea Girl' is good.

Salvias of all kinds have become darlings of the new-look, Mediterranean-meets-the-tropics type of garden. Left to themselves, they mostly peak in late summer, but then continue to look good for a long time through the autumn. Try *Salvia patens* 'Cambridge Blue' or the beefier, more dramatic 'Guanajuato'. Both have the hooked or beaked flowers typical of salvias. They will eventually make tubers, like dahlias. In

*Salvia patens* 'Cambridge Blue', p.166

## Most bedding schemes have too many colours in them. Three is plenty. Two is better.

a mild winter these will survive in the ground. Where winters are severe, you will have to lift the tubers and store them, as you would dahlias, in a frost-free shed for the winter.

Use the salvia with a feathery argyranthemum such as pale, chalky yellow 'Jamaica Primrose', or pale pink-flowered 'Vancouver'. These are not hardy either, but the whole point of these bedding schemes is that they are temporary installations, to be renewed and changed according to one's fancy. For the centrepiece, try a plant such as *Plumbago auriculata*, more often seen as a climber than a standard. In Mediterranean climates, it will overwinter outside, but otherwise will have to be sheltered in a conservatory. The foliage is instantly forgettable but the flowers are a charming shade of ice-blue, simple in outline, like those of a jasmine.

For a variation on the blue and silver theme, combine a blue-flowered salvia with pyrethrum (*Tanacetum coccineum*) and use a tall standard helichrysum to give height to the group. *Salvia farinacea* 'Victoria' has spikes of rich violet-blue flowers on stems which are an even more intense and deep blue. It is easy to raise from seed, but in a sunless summer, maddeningly late to come into flower. With it, use a pyrethrum such as 'Silver Feather' which will make a filigree edging to the bed. It grows no higher than 30cm (12in). To add a subtle dash of greenish yellow, choose

**Summer's glow**
*Though it is not reliably hardy,*
Stachys albotomentosa
*produces lovely spikes of soft
red flowers, whorled around
the strong stems in the same
way as those of the more
common lamb's ear. Mixed
with the stachys are the yellow
daisy flowers of* Bidens
ferulifolia *'Golden Goddess'.
This is a short-lived perennial,
commonly treated as an
annual.*

*Helichrysum petiolare* 'Limelight' for your centrepiece, trained up a bamboo cane to make a mop-headed standard. It is a much more interesting plant than plain silver helichrysum, though the foliage may burn in intense sun.

## BEDDING SCHEMES FOR SHADE

Although annuals generally relish full sun, you can also, if you choose carefully, create quick bedding schemes in areas that are partly shaded. *Impatiens* (busy Lizzie) and lobelia will both put up with shade (indeed

*If you think busy Lizzies are stylistically beyond the pale..... prepare yourself for a revelation. They are invaluable plants.*

impatiens relishes it, provided it is not too starved and dry). Try for instance an impatiens such as 'Accent White' or some other white-flowered type, with bright blue-flowered lobelia, either the dark or the pale blue version. The dark-flowered one, which has dark overlays on the foliage too, will make the better association. Both can easily be raised from seed and both will flower their hearts out from early summer until killed by frost.

Unfortunately, busy Lizzies invite prejudice. You might have spent your whole gardening life avoiding them, thinking them stylistically beyond the pale. You might feel your whole value-system would crash if even the most innocuous busy Lizzie found a toe-hold on your patch. Prepare yourself for a revelation. They are invaluable plants, easy (which may be why they are so often despised) disease-resistant, long-flowering and, it can't be stressed enough, excellent in deep shade. The best effects come from using plants all of the same colour, instead of mixtures. You might use white, as above, or a variety such as 'Jumbo Mauve', an easy colour to live with – deep pink, streaked and gently floured over with white. Whoever named it has got a funny idea of mauve. The jumbo bit must come from the fact that it grows 30cm (12in) tall, but stands upright even in stormy weather. Each little plant will throw up at least a dozen stems and flower fit to bust.

Busy Lizzies are mostly bred from wild species of impatiens that grow in East Africa and Zanzibar, but 'Jumbo Mauve' is like the wild impatiens that grow along stream banks in Costa Rica. These are tall, rangy plants, that flourish in deep shade. That is not true of many showy annuals. Remembering their damp homes in Zanzibar, you need to keep them well watered. Then they will win you over by their grace. Avoid dwarf types. Too often, we are fed squat busy Lizzies that have no presence at all. And too often, they are sold in mixed colours.

### Cool zone

*Summer in the garden does not necessarily mean bright colour. This cool combination includes the scalloped leaves of the plume poppy (Macleaya cordata), the barley-like heads of a perennial grass, Hordeum jubatum, white tobacco flowers and the crinkled foliage of curly kale.*

Much depends on choosing the right colour. There are some vile introductions, as indeed there are in any plant family where breeders have meddled too much. Avoid 'Seashells Yellow' if ever you should come across it. The flowers are indeed yellowish when they first come out, but as they age, the colour bleaches to an unpleasant flesh tone, flushed from the centre outwards with a bilious pink.

Use busy Lizzies in a damp, shady spot in the garden, perhaps with 'Non Stop' begonias. Anyone who grows begonias as house plants knows what good leaves they have. Think of 'Burle Marx' or *Begonia manicata*. The same is true of the begonias you can use outside: the foliage of the 'Non Stop' begonias is characteristically lopsided, hairy, healthy-looking and like the busy Lizzies, excellent in shade. Like busy Lizzies, 'Non Stop' begonias are often offered in mixed colours. But the best effects come from choosing a single colour, perhaps a softish pink with not too much salmon in it, a shade deeper or paler than the busy Lizzies. The flowers are like waxy poppies. Two enormous petals curve round in an outer cup, with the rest of the petals bunched up to make a double flower within. At least, the boss flower is a double. Where the stem has more than one bloom, the outriders are single, but in exactly the same colour.

*Geranium palmatum*, p.82

To complete the exotic, slightly unreal effect that these plants create in a garden, add to them a statuesque plant such as *Geranium palmatum*. It will provide a contrast of form and foliage, fountaining up in the middle of the group. This slightly tender geranium is evergreen and early into new growth. Already by early spring, its great palmate leaves will be there, ready to set off groups of tulips, which you might use to fill the ground in spring, before the busy Lizzies and begonias can be put in place. *Geranium maderense* is similar, but more tender.

## QUINTESSENTIAL SUMMER ANNUALS

Two flowers in particular capture the brilliance and fleetingness of summer: poppies and zinnias. In their bright petals, the summer garden is distilled. Both are easy to grow in full sun and light, well-drained soil. Both provide an incredibly diverse set of possibilities for a gardener. Shirley poppies, for instance, selected from the wild Flanders poppy, *Papaver rhoeas*, can be yellow, pink, orange, red, white, smudgy mauve, double or single. All are enchanting. The name sounds as if it might have come from some Templesque girl, given to floating chiffon. Not so. The flowers are the

creation of the Reverend William Wilks, one of those fortunate nineteenth-century English clergymen whose gardening took precedence over everything else in their lives. Wilks was the vicar of Shirley, near Croydon in Surrey, and created the strain from a single white-edged poppy growing among the wild, plain red ones in a corner of his vicarage garden.

Wilks marked the flower, and the following year raised two hundred plants from the single head of seed. He rogued his plants severely, and for 20 years selected only the best of the seedlings to grow on. In this laborious way, he created a strain of poppies in a wide range of colours, that look like tissue paper left out in the rain. "I am about my flowers between three and four o'clock in the morning," he wrote, "so as to pull up and trample on the bad ones before the bees have a chance of conveying pollen to others."

There are other excellent seed strains of *Papaver rhoeas* such as 'Mother of Pearl', which produces fragile, double-flowered Shirley poppies in fabulous bruised colours, dirty greyish pink, Victorian dove mauve, some colours with a picotee edge of a paler colour round their petals. Rain does

## Painting with poppies

*In the right conditions, this annual field poppy, Papaver rhoeas 'Mother of Pearl', is a vigorous self-seeder. The strain was raised by the painter Sir Cedric Morris in his garden at Benton End, Suffolk. As well as red, flowers can be grey, dirty pink or lavender, many of them double.*

*Papaver rhoeas* 'Mother of Pearl', p.208

not suit them, but we can at least hope that in this period of high summer sun will subdue showers. By selecting and saving seed from flowers with the colours you like best, you can continue to fine-tune a seed mixture to your own ends, abandoning the wishy-washy colours you don't like and strengthening the shades you want. You can do it with other poppies too, such as the Iceland poppies, *Papaver nudicaule*. They are neater plants than the rangy Shirley poppies, the flowers rising from a basal rosette of finely cut leaves, not hairy like *P. rhoeas*, but faintly glaucous.

The Shirley poppies are at the blue end of the red spectrum, the Iceland poppies on the yellow side. But, again, by endlessly selecting and sowing your own seed of the Iceland poppy, you can create your own mixtures of creams and apricots and pinks, eliminating, if you want, the bright yellows and oranges of the original species.

## On a blue note

*This is a simple combination, but an effective and elegant one. Round pepperpot seedheads of the biennial poppy* Papaver somniferum, *in glaucous grey, contrast with the blue-green foliage and purple flowers of* Cerinthe major *'Purpurascens'.*

When you have collected and cleaned the seed, you should sow it in a 12cm (5in) pot, just pressing it into the surface of the compost. Cover the pot with clingfilm and put a slate or something similar over it to keep out the light until the seedlings have germinated. Prick out the seedlings into 7cm (3in) pots and grow them on before setting out the plants in early autumn. That is the laborious way. If you have light sandy soil and a lucky streak, you can just crush the seedheads and wave them over the patch you want to cover. Take with a pinch of salt any seedsman's claim that these poppies "will come up year after year in the garden".

*Annual flowers are essential components of a summer border.....they are the curlicues, the garnishes in a garden.*

Easier in that respect are the opium poppies, varieties of *Papaver somniferum*. On heavy, damp soil, these are the most trouble-free of all the annual and biennial poppies. Where they are happy, plants will grow 1.2m (4ft) tall, with masses of buds, minding the wet less than the Shirley poppies. The leaves are handsome, the best of all the poppies, rich, waxy, silvery. The common kind has deep purple flowers with dark smudges at the bottom of the petals, which are ranged around a ring of pale cream stamens. Bumblebees come stumbling out of the flowers covered in white pollen. But other colours crop up, too – a deep, almost black poppy, a beautiful magenta with purple smudges, a rich red – and these are worth perpetuating by seed. The seedlings of good forms often have leaves that are more intricately edged (as if they have been cut with pinking shears) than the ordinary kinds. The flowers don't last long, but the seedheads are dramatic, much better than those of either the Shirley or the Iceland poppies. When the foliage starts to get drab and scrappy, you can pull up the opium poppies that you don't want, leaving the best ones to self-seed. Some of the opium poppies make great powderpuff flowers, doubles such as 'Pink Chiffon', or the dramatic 'Black Peony' (the name describes it exactly).

*Papaver somniferum* 'Paeony Flowered', p.102

### Ruffed up

*The bracts surrounding the domed heads of the fine sea holly* Eryngium alpinum *are soft yet spiny at the same time. It has the largest flowers of this tribe, all of which are brilliant garden plants. The airy pale flowers of* Gillenia trifoliata *float insubstantially around it.*

*Zinnia* Allsorts, p.168

Zinnias are much more outrageous flowers than poppies, so self-evidently foreign and exotic, gardeners automatically assume that they must be difficult to grow. But no. Seed will germinate generously within four days. The only difficulty may be that you will have sown it too early. Zinnias hate to be checked. Once started into growth, they like to zoom helter-skelter onwards. But they also hate frost. If you live in the kind of place where tender plants cannot go out until late spring or early summer, you may have to keep them champing at the bit too long indoors.

When the seedlings have made their first proper set of leaves, transplant each one into a separate 7cm (3in) pot and grow them on until you can harden them off and set them in place outside. They make big, bushy plants that come into flower in high summer. They will still be flowering in autumn and are fabulous enough to upstage even a dahlia. Upstaging a dahlia, when you are only a tenth of its size, is a cheeky thing to do. There are many different seed strains to choose from. Purists look down on

## *Thinking only of colour can blind you to the rest of a plant's attributes — or its faults.*

mixtures such as Allsorts, but if you want to understand what tricks a flower can do, growing a mixture is the easiest way to learn. Some plants will produce vast footballs of flowers, shocking pink, orange and yellow. Some are an extraordinary chartreuse green. Some have wonderfully complex centres, the stamens ringed in contrasting colours. Few are duffers.

Start your selection process by discounting any variety that the seedsman describes as a "dwarf strain". By nature, zinnias make wonderfully muscular, meaty growth, which does not need support. The overall habit is robust and the stems are strong. Other, weakly constructed plants may be strengthened by dwarfing. Zinnias do not need it. So do not go anywhere near a variety called 'Starbright Mixed'. You may have thought it impossible to invent an ugly zinnia. You are wrong. Here is a skinny, mean dwarf, with flowers smaller than a single French marigold

## Sparring partners

*Tall cream spires of* Cimicifuga simplex *fight for supremacy with the yellow sunflower* Helianthus *'Capenoch Star'. The blue monkshood* Aconitum carmichaelii *'Kelmscott' is the recessive colour in this group, which is dominated by a fine spread of the zinnia 'Giant Flowered Mix'.*

in a limited and hideous range of colours (mostly a harsh orange). What a waste, when you could have been growing the ice-green zinnia 'Envy', which is gorgeous, 60cm (24in) high, with lime-green flowers. 'Tufted Exemption' has odd, almost conical heads, with a lower row of petals making a frill around the bottom. 'Scabious Flowered' has huge, crested flowers in a mixture of scarlet, carmine, pink, yellow, orange and cream.

The first zinnia to arrive in this country was *Zinnia pauciflora*. Its name suggests it was an unimpressive performer, and Phillip Miller, who grew it in the Chelsea Physic Garden, London, in the 1750s, was not enthusiastic about it. Most of today's garden varieties have been bred from another Mexican species, *Z. elegans*. This was being grown in Britain by 1796, thanks to the Marchioness of Bute, wife of the Ambassador to the Spanish court. She had been given it by Professor Ortega of Madrid, who also supplied her with the first dahlias to be seen in Britain.

## THINKING ABOUT COLOUR

For some people, the colours of a troupe of brilliant salsa-playing zinnias will be too strong. They are also likely to shy away from a garden border planted with a solid mass of oriental poppies, in shades of orange-red, red-red, and pink-red. Views on colour are one of the most instantly articulated expressions of taste. We register it, we have views on it, more quickly and more certainly than on any other aspect of our surroundings. But the thing about gardens is that they shift all the time. For a short spell, a poppy border may well be an all-red border. But when they are over, the border can shift into a completely different gear, perhaps majoring in tall tobacco plants in cool lime green and white.

Single colour borders, that is, borders that stick to one colour throughout the year, seem to be an easy option. They seem to offer a way of avoiding difficult decisions about what goes with what. But they're much more difficult to do well than mixed borders. A blue flower doesn't necessarily go with another flower that is also blue. It may look very much better against a white flower or a yellow one.

This is true for instance of the veronica called 'Crater Lake Blue' and *Campanula latifolia*. Both are blue, but the veronica is an intense, brilliant true blue while the campanula is a drifty, mauveish, much more recessive blue. Together they look awful. The veronica, being a clean, straight colour can take another clean colour nearby, white moon daisies or the clear yellow of daisy-flowered *Chrysanthemum segetum* (corn marigold). The campanula sings in a minor key and needs other un-primary colours with it: dirty pink astrantias, deep purplish clematis, lime-green tobacco flowers.

White is one of the most difficult colours to handle effectively. Vita Sackville-West made it look dangerously easy at Sissinghurst, her garden in Kent. But the dead chalk white of a plant such as sweet rocket is hideous if used next to the much creamier white of a rose such as 'Nevada'. In a garden setting, the creamy whites are much more easy-going than dead whites. They do not draw the eye so insistently. They are accommodating neighbours. The dead whites can often only be used in a single mass, set perhaps against a dark green hedge, with little else in view. The white of sweet rocket is a stark, harsh, straight white and these straight colours are harder to place properly than oblique, off-beam ones, such as white foxgloves, which, when you look at them, are actually slightly creamy, greeny.

## Hazy days

*A misty purplish blue, soft and appealing, knits together these two partners, Allium cristophii and Nepeta 'Six Hills Giant'. This is a prolific catmint, which contributes to the garden for a long period, through the whole of summer.*

*Lilium regale, p.166*

*Verbascum chaixii* 'Gainsborough', p.176

Gertrude Jekyll preached that white flowers should be set off by touches of blue or lemon-yellow, a gospel followed by the great gardener Phyllis Reiss, at Tintinhull in Somerset, where the white flowers in the Fountain Garden were thrown into relief against grey-blue and acid yellow.

The American gardener Lawrence Johnston's "white" garden at Hidcote in Gloucestershire is similarly subtle. He didn't choose a dead-white rose to fill the beds there but 'Gruss an Aachen', which has creamy flowers overlaid with soft pink. The white osteospermums and the white tobacco plants used in the garden are also both slightly off-beam. The one is overlaid with blue, the other with green. And the pale colours glow there against the dark backdrop of clipped yew and box. White gardens are infinitely more effective in shade than in sun.

But how limiting single colour gardens are. If you have masses of space, then it is no hardship to set aside a corner for a white garden or a swathe of wall for a blue border. But most gardeners don't have space. They want

*Views on colour are one of the most instantly articulated expressions of taste.*

different parts of the garden to feel different, but single colour groupings cut out too many options and often fail to make plants sing as well as they should. The white-flowered Regale lily, for instance, is a brilliant plant, the flowers held in elegant trumpets round the stem. But if you put this cool beauty in front of a white-flowered campanula in a regulation white display, the two things just melt into each other.

But if you try the same plant in a mixed group with the variegated foliage of the phlox 'Norah Leigh', the dark-leaved euphorbia, 'Chameleon' and (at a safe distance) the anchusa 'Loddon Royalist', you get a far richer and better effect. You could add spires of the verbascum 'Gainsborough' to come into lemon-yellow flower when the euphorbia splutters to a finish. That might set your heart beating faster than any white garden ever has – even VS-W's.

The purple border at Sissinghurst is more interesting than the white, because it encompasses every colour from red through to deep blue. In

autumn, the scarlet hips of the 'Geranium' rose (a hybrid from *Rosa moyesii*) are the best things in the border, adding great punches of vitality into what otherwise could be quite a heavy scheme. There are wine-purple alliums, magenta geraniums, deep blue salvias and pale *Clematis* 'Perle d'Azur' with irises and asters, penstemons and a touch – not too much – of purple foliage from the smoke bush, *Cotinus coggygria* 'Foliis Purpureis'.

It's an imposing scheme, but not one that is necessarily easy to live with. It's opera, high-octane stuff. Dark rich tones, such as you get in the leaves of the sedum 'Mohrchen' (where they have a metallic sheen), are less oppressive if leavened with paler colours. The sedum, for instance, looks excellent with the pale striped foliage of *Sisyrinchium striatum* 'Aunt May' and the capricious spurred flowers of a columbine such as *Aquilegia longissima*.

*Aquilegia longissima*, p.78

# A garden that is all flowers is like a cake that is all icing.

Thinking only of colour can blind you to the rest of a plant's attributes – or its faults. Flowering is only one of the tricks that a plant can perform and it is a shorter act than foliage or form. If you garden with single colour borders, you are much more likely to swoop on a plant because it is blue or white or yellow and overlook the fact that its leaves are as inviting as last week's salad and that it holds itself with all the grace of a sailor on a spree. Whether colours "go" will always depend on personal taste. A clamorous border of oriental poppies might be too strong an effect for many gardeners, but the poppies are all on the same side of the line that divides orange-reds from blue-reds. Magenta *Gladiolus communis* subsp. *byzantinus* is on the other side of the divide and looks spectacularly bad with the poppies.

*Gladiolus communis* subsp. *byzantinus*, p.82

The colour of a particular plant can be used to reinforce the lines of a design – or to knit together areas of a garden that are unsatisfactory because of a bad design. Used this way, the colour is more likely to come from foliage than flower. The golden leaves of a hosta can act subtly as a series of signposts through a garden. So can the dark foliage of the herbaceous *Clematis recta* 'Purpurea' or bronze-leaved fennel. For even in high summer, you still need mounds of foliage to set off your flowers, the velvet on which the crown jewels are displayed.

*Clematis recta* 'Purpurea', p.76

## FOLIAGE FRAMEWORK

Flowers Need Foliage. The dictum ought to be scratched in the concrete of every patio in the country, emblazoned on every garden gate, carved on the handle of every garden spade. An obsession with colour has been the distinguishing characteristic of most gardeners who were brought up to revere Sissinghurst with its single colour borders above all other gardens, and to believe that the only true path to the gardener's Nirvana lay through a series of agonized choices about the exact nature of the flowers we put in our patches.

"Darling! Salmon! How brave!" exclaim the white garden brigade as they sharpen their pruning knives for a horticultural mercy killing. You might as well fall on your garden fork there and then as try and explain that the point of the rodgersia they are looking at is not the buff-pink flower but the whirls of bronze underneath it. This obsession with colour and with particular modish flowers has got in the way of a vital tenet of good gardening. Leaves are vastly more important in creating satisfying and enduring planting schemes than flowers. A garden that is all flowers is like a cake that is all icing. And in town gardens, set in the midst of concrete, tarmac, noise, dust and general mayhem, you desperately need cool, still oases of green to set off occasional bursts of colour.

When you first start to garden, you are seduced by flowers. You open a catalogue. You go to a garden centre. You see only the colour of things. You hoover up plants indiscriminately, favouring the ones that are actually in flower at the moment. But being impressed by a plant because of its flowers is like judging a man entirely on the basis of his Armani jacket. Unfortunately, some plants, like some people, have little more to offer and although they may be fine in a crowd, you wouldn't want to spend too much time with them on their own.

Annual flowers are wonderful; they are essential components of a summer garden, but they rarely have impressive leaves and consequently look much better when they can borrow the foliage of other plants than when they are planted on their own. They are the curlicues, the garnishes in the garden, but rarely have enough beef in them to constitute the main course.

To get a sustaining backbone into a garden you need plants that look their best for more than a six-week flowering period. When you swoop on a plant in flower in the garden centre, ask yourself "What will this thing

look like without its flowers? Will it develop an interesting shape? What are its leaves like?" If you judge a plant by these criteria, flowers become a bonus, rather than the sole *raison d'être*. Some of these key backbone plants should be evergreen, so that in winter the garden does not entirely dissolve into a skein of skeletal branches. The spurge *Euphorbia characias* is a great ally in this respect, making solid mounds of evergreen foliage spiralled around stout upright stems. Its main season is spring, but even when, after several months, you finally cut down the spent flowerheads, the foliage lends its splendid sea-green bulk to any summer flowers you might arrange around it. It always enhances, never detracts.

This euphorbia, like the hosta, is a foliage plant with a capital F. Other plants, such as crocosmia, are not so firmly labelled, but although you might leap on it because of its arched sprays of brilliant red flowers you will gradually find that the long, pleated sword-shaped leaves are of equal

*Even in high summer, you still need mounds of foliage to set off your flowers, the velvet on which the crown jewels are displayed.*

consequence. You need these sharp verticals to give variety in plant groups. Use the scarlet crocosmia 'Lucifer' with the dark-leaved dahlia 'Bishop of Llandaff', which has flowers of an equally outrageous colour. You will have chosen both plants on account of their late summer display, but long before either of them comes into flower in high summer you will have had the pleasure of the contrast in foliage.

All foliage has bulk. Not all has beauty. Sometimes you are prepared to trade off boring leaves for the sake of some other attribute, such as scent. There may be something about the smell of the plant's flowers that makes you suspend judgement on its other qualities. You float on that smell. You feel good about the world. You love your neighbour. For that, you are prepared to let slip a leaf that is no more than leafish. This is not to say that you should have nothing in your garden that you could not defend in front of a foliage tribunal. Only that you should

### All the blues
*Love-in-a-mist* (Nigella damascena) *pays rent three times over in the garden, first with its fine, thread-like foliage, then with enchanting sky blue flowers, finally with conspicuous greenish seedheads. In this combination of moody blues it is partnered by* Clematis integrifolia *and* Geranium *'Johnson's Blue'.*

*Crocosmia* 'Lucifer', p.146

## Quiet elegance

*The creamy colour on the variegated leaves of* Hosta *'Wide Brim' is echoed in the flowers of* Verbascum chaixii *'Gainsborough', borne on tall branching stems. The young foliage of* Stachys byzantina *'Primrose Heron' also has a distinctive pale yellow overlay, which fades away as the leaves age.*

*Rodgersia aesculifolia,* p.174, and *R. pinnata* 'Superba', p.90

*Matteuccia struthiopteris,* p.152
*Adiantum aleuticum,* p.202

have a good reason for including anything that would not stand up in such a court.

Where, as with the crocosmia, you get foliage and flowers of equal value, you are in clover (another double act). These are the plants to favour. Rodgersia is another winner. It is often portrayed as a bog plant, but is perfectly happy in ordinary soil, provided it is not a dust bowl. There is not a dud in the whole family. The flowers come out in this season, showy, plush plumes of pink or white, but the plants have already paid two months' garden rent with their leaves, which are outstanding.

*Rodgersia aesculifolia* has glossy bronze foliage, the leaflets radiating out like the spokes of an umbrella from a central stalk, the end of each leaflet bluntly cut like a horse chestnut leaf. *Rodgersia pinnata* has leaves similarly arranged, but without the gloss. The leaflets do not have the same blunt end and the plant generally is less massively built. Ferns are natural companions, either the tall shuttlecock fern, *Matteuccia struthiopteris*, or the more delicately built maidenhair fern, *Adiantum aleuticum*. So is the grass *Pennisetum*, with its caterpillar seedheads.

### PLAYING WITH PURPLE

But some foliage needs to be used with a light hand. Purple is the trickiest, because it can give an over-heavy, saturated effect, if used in the great wodges that purple berberis, or purple nut thrust upon the eye. Fortunately, this book does not deal with shrubs, so we need not worry about them here. But purple has become very trendy, especially when combined with equally rich colours such as royal blue and cardinal red. The problem with trends is that by the time most of us have caught up with them, the people who set them have moved on to something else. So one is always one step behind, never quite in the right place at the right time.

In this case, since there are so many good plants with purple foliage or purple flowers, we might hope that this is more than a trend and that purple is here to stay. When the Next Big Thing comes along, sensible gardeners will hang on to their purple iris, their alliums, tulips, hellebores, sweet Williams and fritillaries. They are good plants. Every garden should have them. Even in minimalist gardens, where only spiky things or isolated clumps of plants with green flowers are allowed to sully the clear, swept expanses of concrete and smooth sheets of aluminium, purple has found

## Heads and tails

*A simple partnership, but an effective one, with the strange conical heads of* Allium sphaerocephalon *dancing around with seedheads of the opium poppy,* Papaver somniferum, *and the fluffy topknots of the hare's tail grass,* Lagurus ovatus.

*Allium giganteum*, p.138

*Allium cristophii*, p.140

its place. It goes very well with grey. It can be called a "statement". It has more angst than white.

Alliums, particularly, are designer darlings. All are built on roughly the same lines, a stem with a blob on top and most, but not all, are purple. The differences have to do with the proportion of stem to blob. *Allium cristophii* is squat, top heavy, with too much blob for its stem, but has sufficient presence to overcome its inbuilt design problem. *Allium caeruleum* has 60cm (24in) of stem, which leads you to expect something rather splendid at the top. In fact the flower is only about 2.5cm (1in) across, but the colour is a good, clear sky blue. If you plant enough of them, the effect is excellent, particularly when they poke through a low sea of something greyish, perhaps a prostrate form of *Artemisia stelleriana*.

*Allium giganteum* is the family's grand slam, footballs balanced on 1.2m (4ft) stems. Even the bulbs are monsters. The flowerheads are similar to *A. cristophii*, but appear later, mid- rather than early summer. The extra height is useful, too. At Hidcote, the National Trust garden in Gloucestershire, these alliums are used down the back of a border of double peonies. They would also make good companions for the supreme foliage plant *Melianthus major*, perhaps with agapanthus to pick up the baton later.

Purple has always been around in gardens, of course. Think of violas, lupins and the beautiful dark-leaved angelica called *A. gigas*. Think of the gorgeous cow parsley called *Anthriscus sylvestris* 'Ravenswing' with its purplish-brown foliage. Or the elegant fountain grass *Pennisetum setaceum*,

*Angelica gigas*, p.90

> *White is not good with purple, but pink is, provided it is the deep and saturated kind.*

with leaves and flowering heads that look as though they have been soaked in claret. So stop overdosing on pastels. We've had more than enough of them. Drifts of grey. Billows of pink. Washing powder white. This is somnambulist gardening. White appeals to those who like everything to be neat and tidy, according to the National Garden Bureau in America, which has been exploring the psychology of colour in gardens. It has nothing to say about purple. Perhaps it was censored. There is something altogether more passionate about purple than white.

White is not good with purple, but pink is, provided it is the deep and saturated kind. Try the inky aquilega 'William Guiness' with sheets of brilliant dianthus in front of it. Try pink bleeding heart, *Dicentra spectabilis*, planted in front of the excellent herbaceous clematis *C. recta* 'Purpurea', which has leaves heavily saturated with purple. Use the dirty purple oriental poppy 'Patty's Plum' with sheaves of the magenta-flowered gladiolus, *G. communis* subsp. *byzantinus*.

*Papaver orientale* 'Patty's Plum', p.94; *Gladiolus communis* subsp. *byzantinus*, p.82

Purple also works with rich royal blues, such as anchusa provides. Hairy anchusa, with its searingly blue flowers, is an unreliable perennial but when you see well-grown plants, they are not easily forgotten. Use them behind purple bearded iris, such as 'Langport Wren' (short) or 'Swazi Princess' (much taller), and combine them with giant alliums. Try bronze fennel to fill in the gaps, or perhaps some first-year plants of purple angelica. Later in the summer season, you could start a purplish group with a plant such as *Verbena bonariensis*, all stem and no leaf. The thin stems branch in an angular way, and at the end of each branch is a tuft of flowers. They start coming out as high summer begins, but are still performing at the onset of winter, their tall, skeletal forms waltzing along with late flowers of *Salvia patens* 'Cambridge Blue'. Although it is tall – up to 1.5m (5ft) – it is so wiry and insubstantial that you can see through it easily. You can use it, like a bead curtain, at the front of a border, to provide a tantalizing screen for something that lies beyond.

> *Often purple-leaved plants can act as the anchor of a group, with more seasonal companions ebbing and flowing around them.*

Among the stems of the verbena you could use one of the scrambling purple-magenta geraniums, such as 'Russell Prichard' or 'Ann Folkard', which would thicken up the mass, but not get in the way of the verbena's flowers. Few garden plants have such a long season of flower as 'Russell Prichard'. It starts in early summer and continues until autumn, when the long, scrambling side-branches die back to the compact, central crown.

Where there is space for it to spread its wide wands of flower, use dierama by the verbena, or instead of it. You must get the tall kind, *Dierama pulcherrimum*, with flowering stems that make great arcs bending away from the central clumps of grassy leaves. 'Blackbird' has exceptionally dark flowers, wine purple, fairly sinister. The buds emerge from dry, buff paper cases and hang on threads so fine that you cannot see them.

In the garden, purple plants work best when they are set against other colours which throw them into relief. But which colours? Purple does not work with white, because the contrast is harsh, unsympathetic. But it works with cream, with orange (if you are really brave) and best of all with its sister colours red, deep pink and blue. Often purple-leaved plants can act as the anchor of a group, with more seasonal companions ebbing and flowing around them. Sometimes, as with the superb foliage plant *Rheum palmatum* 'Atrosanguineum' the purples themselves ebb and flow. Rheum is a posh kind of rhubarb with gorgeous, great, jagged leaves. In spring it is mesmerizing: great clenched fists of buds, glossy and impatient. The flowers shoot up, panicles of purplish red, towards late spring. Then it collapses. Totally. But you can quickly fill the gap with summer purples, cannas such as 'Roi Humbert', perhaps. Or you could move in a dahlia such as 'Arabian Night' with flowers that are practically black. The foliage is green. Even better is 'Grenadier' where the purple rests in the leaves and the flowers are rich, singing red. Neither canna nor dahlia can go out until frosts are a thing of the past, so in fact it is very selfless of the rheum to pack itself away at exactly the right time for the new troops to come in.

*Dahlia* 'Grenadier', p.204

*Artemisia lactiflora* Guizhou Group will give you more permanent summer effects, feathery mounds of well-cut leaves drowned in purple. In late spring, you will have only the artemisia's foliage to play around with. You might splash purple tulips round it – 'Negrita' or cream and purple 'Shirley'. Later in summer, when the artemisia is enormous – up to 1.5m (5ft) – with heads of creamy-white flowers, you might look for pink lilies to set in pots in front of it.

In the end, it's all about weight. You don't want too much of it, which is why it is a grave mistake to jam a load of purple plants together, unleavened by other colours. And you need to be more careful with purple foliage than you do with flowers. The flowers are evanescent. The foliage will be with you for months. But never be afraid to gamble. The unexpected success is far sweeter than a certainty. □

# Allium giganteum *with* Anemone x hybrida 'Königen Charlotte' *and* Atriplex hortensis var. rubra

Spherical heads are the defining feature of these summer-flowering members of the onion family. They are made up of masses of tiny star-shaped flowers in various shades of purplish pink. *Allium giganteum*, as its name suggests, is one of the tallest of the tribe and has densely packed heads of purple flowers. The thin strappy leaves have a grey tinge and droop at the ends. They are susceptible to spring frosts. This allium needs a sheltered, sunny spot and well-drained soil. Heavy soil can be improved with coarse sand or grit, mixed in the planting hole. Do not cut back the foliage, but allow it to die down naturally. It feeds goodness back into the bulbs for the next season. Remember that when an allium's flower is at its best, its foliage will already be dying back and looking scrappy. You need to arrange them so they float, like extraterrestrials, over a sea of borrowed foliage such as that supplied by the orache and anemone. Kindly, they will disguise the allium's quietly rotting leaves.

## Allium giganteum
**Height** *1.5–2m (5–6ft).*
**Spread** *15cm (6in).*
**Flowering time** *Early to midsummer.*
**Star qualities** *Stylish, architectural outline. Striking spherical heads of deep lilac flowers. Strong stems that do not need staking.*
**Other varieties** Allium hollandicum *grows to 1m (3ft) with dense heads of purplish-pink flowers;* 'Globemaster' *grows to 80cm (32in) with enormous heads of deep violet flowers.*

### Atriplex hortensis var. rubra (Red orache)
*Orache is a leafy annual, which in this variety produces plants up to 1.2m (4ft) tall with pointed leaves of a rich, saturated purple. It flowers, but the main point of the plant is its foliage. It can become a nuisance as seeds scatter and germinate very freely. Be warned. Take your revenge by eating surplus seedlings. The orache's other common name is mountain spinach. Use it to give bite to a summer salad.*

### Anemone x hybrida 'Königin Charlotte' (Japanese anemone)
*Japanese anemones are tough, hardy creatures thriving in a wide range of conditions. The growth is strongly upright and the foliage relatively sparse. 'Königin Charlotte' is an exceptionally vigorous variety and will reach 1.5m (5ft). In late summer and autumn, it has large, semi-double pink flowers, each one 10cm (4in) across. The backs of the petals are stained with purple.*

*Allium giganteum*

# Astrantia major 'Shaggy' *with* Allium cristophii *and* Galtonia candicans

Used with more ephemeral, showy companions, this handsome astrantia will give pleasure for at least six months of the year. By mid-autumn it will be looking distinctly shabby and it is best to shear down the foliage then, ready for a fresh start in spring. The hand-shaped leaves are deeply cut and make sturdy, vigorous clumps. By early summer you will already be seeing the charming, papery flowerheads, which stand in good condition for many weeks. The astrantia is the anchor in this group, its pale, elegant flowers enlivened first by the purple globes of the allium, whose own foliage it can disguise, and then by the late summer flowers of the galtonia, purer and whiter than those of the astrantia with their greenish underlay can ever be. The bulbs have no *raison d'être* but their flowers. The astrantia gives necessary bulk and longevity to the group.

## Astrantia major 'Shaggy' (Masterwort)
**Height** *30–90cm (12–36in)*.
**Spread** *45cm (18in)*.
**Flowering time** *Early to midsummer.*
**Star qualities** *Strange, papery greenish-white bracts, very long in this variety, surround tiny greenish-white flowers. Each flowerhead looks like a miniature posy.*
**Other varieties** *'Hadspen Blood' has dark red bracts surrounding dark red pinpoint flowers; 'Sunningdale Variegated' has pale pink bracts surrounding greenish flowers held above handsome leaves strongly variegated in creamy yellow.*

## Allium cristophii
*This allium needs hot, dry conditions and is fussy about drainage, but it is worth the fuss because it is extremely showy both in flower and after, when the whole head has bleached to a creamy straw colour. It takes a long time to fall apart. The individual flowers have six narrow petals, but you tend not to see them as individuals. The mass is what matters, the whole construction like a geodesic dome, about 18cm (7in) across.*

## Galtonia candicans
*Galtonia is a native of South Africa's eastern Cape, where it gets rain in summer and lies dormant in winter. It is not always easy to establish, but once you see its deliciously waxy white bells, like those of an overgrown summer hyacinth, you want to make every effort to please it. Plant bulbs in early spring, setting them at least 15cm (6in) deep. Cut down the flowered stems in autumn. Galtonias are slow to increase, but ground well enriched with rotted compost will help them on their way.*

*Astrantia major* 'Shaggy' ▷

# Campanula latiloba 'Hidcote Amethyst' *with* Centranthus ruber *and* Alchemilla mollis

The standard types of border campanulas, *C. latiloba*, *C. latifolia* and their like, are not fussy about soil, though in the wild, most are found on alkaline soil. They are also very tolerant of shade, though again, left to themselves, they would choose a spot that was in sun for at least part of the day. They enjoy being split and replanted in fresh ground every couple of years. They do not need lush feeding – they are used to fighting for survival – and are wonderfully resilient against pests and diseases. The blues of the border campanulas are misty and diluted, excellent with valerian (*Centranthus*), either of the pink or the white sort. The lime-green heads of the alchemilla will froth round underneath the two taller components of this group, a classic trio for a summer cottage garden.

## Campanula latiloba 'Hidcote Amethyst'

**Height** *90cm (36in).*
**Spread** *45cm (18in).*
**Flowering time** *Mid- to late summer.*
**Star qualities** *Pale amethyst flowers, shaded with deeper purple. Strong, ground-hugging rosettes of lance-shaped leaves.*
**Other varieties** C. latiloba *'Percy Piper' has lavender-blue flowers; C. 'Burghaltii' has bell-shaped greyish-blue flowers in midsummer; C.* lactiflora *'Prichard's Variety' grows to 75cm (30in) with violet-blue flowers from early summer to early autumn.*

### Centranthus ruber (Valerian)

*This is such a common plant, naturalizing easily in walls and wild areas of the garden, that it is easily overlooked. But it is invaluable in creating a relaxed, cottage-style effect in a garden. The flowers, carried in rounded heads, are usually pink, though a fine white form also exists. The height is rarely more than 1.2m (4ft) and the plant lolls on its elbows, spreading to about 40–80cm (16–32in).*

### Alchemilla mollis

*Alchemilla ranks as one of the most useful of all ground-covering plants, common, but indispensable. Its only vice is an over-enthusiastic urge to procreate. Be ruthless with self-sown seedlings, or avoid them altogether by cutting down the flowerheads before they seed. The leaves are shallowly lobed and fairly hairy. Their most endearing characteristic is the way they hold drops of water, rolling them round like small balls of mercury.*

*Campanula latiloba* 'Hidcote Amethyst' ▷

# Cerinthe major 'Purpurascens' *with* Hosta 'Lemon Lime' *and* Triteleia laxa

Cerinthe took the gardening world by storm when this luscious purple-flowered form, originally a native of the Mediterranean area, was reintroduced in an improved form from New Zealand. It is an annual and though it self-seeds, the seedlings are not always tough enough to make it through winter. Cerinthe is used to a Mediterranean climate, and will certainly be able to look after itself in areas which do not have frost in winter. Otherwise, you will have to raise fresh plants from seed each year, to perpetuate the stock. The hosta, when it arrives, will give bulk to the group and a long succession of mauve flowers that will tone with the cerinthe's own, bizarre flowerheads. But this group has nothing for winter. That may not matter, especially if there is a clump of *Euphorbia amygdaloides* var. *robbiae* or some other evergreen nearby to take your eye away from the gap. Triteleia gives an enchanting lift in midsummer.

**Cerinthe major 'Purpurascens'**
**Height** *60cm (24in).*
**Spread** *30cm (12in).*
**Flowering time** *Early to late summer.*
**Star qualities** *Fleshy, slightly glaucous foliage. Strange drooping flowerheads that sometimes seem steely grey, sometimes ultramarine, mauve or purple, saturated and exotic.*
**Other varieties** *The standard species has pale, grey-green leaves, blotched with white, and bluish bracts enclosing tubular yellow flowers.*

### Triteleia laxa

*Think of an agapanthus, shrunk in the wash, and you will have some idea of what this plant looks like. Loose clusters of tubular blue flowers spring from stalks which can be up to 60cm (24in) high. They flower in midsummer, just before agapanthus, and, being natives of California, like warm, sunny spots in the garden. Plant the corms about 8cm (3in) deep in autumn.*

### Hosta 'Lemon Lime'

*The only problem with hostas is that slugs dote on them as much as gardeners do. Prepare to defend the lush spikes when they first push through the ground. There are hundreds of varieties to choose from; this one has dainty foliage, no more than 8cm (3in) long. It grows vigorously, with leaves that are yellow at the tips, shading to lime towards the stalks. A succession of purplish flowers, striped with white, are produced in summer on stems 30cm (12in) long.*

*Cerinthe major* 'Purpurascens' ▷

# Crocosmia 'Lucifer' *with* Hemerocallis 'Stafford' *and* Tropaeolum majus 'Empress of India'

Crocosmia leaves are almost as good as those of an iris, though they do not have quite the same stiff, upright formality and they are a greener green, without that glaucous overlay that makes the iris stand out so well. But the crocosmia has something the iris doesn't have: ribbing, made by the pleats running lengthways down the leaf. These long ribs are the plant's scaffolding. Even in spring, crocosmia leaves are advanced and handsome enough to make useful landmarks between camassias and mounds of brunnera. When the crocosmia flowers, with its brilliant crimson sprays, it will be partnered by the day lily (*Hemerocallis*), a richer, brickier kind of red. Both will be outlasted by the nasturtiums, which charge on into autumn with wonderfully reckless abandon. Hungry gardeners should note that buds of day lily and leaves of nasturtium are good to eat. So are nasturtium seeds when green and peppery.

### *Crocosmia* 'Lucifer'
**Height** *1–1.2m (3–4ft).*
**Spread** *75cm (30in).*
**Flowering time** *Mid- to late summer.*
**Star qualities** *Robust habit of growth; brilliant red flowers, much bigger and more effective than old kinds of "monbretia"; handsome pleated leaves.*
**Other varieties** *C. x crocosmiiflora 'Solfatare' has bronze leaves and apricot flowers and 'Gerbe d'Or' has clear lemon-yellow flowers; C. masoniorum has mid-green leaves and orange-red flowers.*

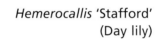

### *Hemerocallis* 'Stafford' (Day lily)

*Day lilies are bomb proof, which endears them to gardeners. Their trumpet flowers are their speciality, but the bright green leaves, emerging early in the year, provide an invaluable foil for spring flowers which may not have much leaf of their own. Yellow day lilies have the strongest scent, usually a good reason for choosing that colour. In this scene, something earthier is called for and 'Stafford' has wonderful scarlet flowers with yellow centres.*

### *Tropaeolum majus* 'Empress of India' (Nasturtium)

*This is a bushy nasturtium, not a climbing one, and it has wonderful foliage of deep blue-green. Nothing could be a better background for the flowers which are deep blood red, sumptuous and velvety. It is the most lustrous and beautiful of all nasturtiums.*

Crocosmia 'Lucifer'

# Delphinium grandiflorum 'Blue Butterfly'
*with* Cosmos bipinnatus 'Sonata White' *and* Lupinus 'Thundercloud'

The vast Pacific Hybrid delphiniums, with spikes up to 2m (6ft) are showy, but not the easiest plants to use in a garden. They are top heavy and require firm staking. Easier in mixed groups are the looser, airier Belladonna types, or *Delphinium grandiflorum*, which is a short-lived perennial. The blue of delphiniums can scarcely be matched by any other flower. It is a clear, clean blue, beautifully set off against its own pale green foliage. If you use delphiniums with white cosmos and spikes of purple lupin, the effect will be cool and restrained. Changing the scheme to include pink cosmos instead of white, will warm up the whole design. This is very much a summer group. All the flowers will be out together, but when they have finished, there will be nothing for autumn or spring. You could fill the spring gap by adding sweetly scented jonquils or bluebells around the newly emerging foliage of the lupins.

### *Delphinium grandiflorum* 'Blue Butterfly'

**Height** *50cm (20in).*
**Spread** *30cm (12in).*
**Flowering time** *Early to mid-summer.*
**Star qualities** *Light, airy growth with flowers of a clear, bright blue. Ferny foliage. More natural in style than the monster spikes of exhibition delphiniums.*
**Other varieties** *D. grandiflorum 'White Butterfly' is similarly airy in growth but has white flowers. The Belladonna Group of delphiniums, which includes cultivars such as 'Cliveden Beauty', are also light and open in growth, but much taller.*

### *Cosmos bipinnatus* 'Sonata White'

*This is an annual that looks as though it should be a perennial, with finely cut foliage and showy, saucer-shaped flowers. The Sonata Series produces flowers that are shorter than most cosmos. It is suggested here because it will match the shortish delphinium in height. But if you use a taller delphinium, perhaps one of the Belladonna group, you could use a bigger cosmos, such as one of the Sensation Series, which grow to 90cm (36in).*

### *Lupinus* 'Thundercloud'

*Lupins have foliage which is as good as their flowers, the leaves deeply cut into a round whorl of leaflets, joined together at the stem. Their heyday was the Fifties, when lupins raised by George Russell of York were a stately component of many herbaceous borders. After the main spike has finished flowering in midsummer, side spikes continue the display for several more weeks.*

*Delphinium grandiflorum*
'Blue Butterfly'

# Dianthus 'Dad's Favourite' *with* Lagurus ovatus *and* Aquilegia 'Hensol Harebell'

Only the dianthus in this group will make a mark for 12 months of the year. The mats of foliage may become slightly weatherbeaten through winter, but in spring, new shoots will freshen the plants and accompany the emerging foliage of the aquilegias. The early effect will be pale grey–green, shattered in midsummer when the dianthus produces its show-stopping purple and white blooms. It's an old-fashioned "laced pink"; each petal is outlined in the same contrasting colour that fills the centre of the flower. In terms of flowers, this is a midsummer group, but deadheading the dianthus should produce occasional flowers later in the season. The aquilegia needs to be cut down when it has finished flowering. It will make fresh mounds of foliage which will be useful fillers between the less substantial stems of the hare's tail grass. Although this is an annual, it has a long season and even in autumn, the fluffy terminal spikes will still be intriguing enough to demand attention.

**Dianthus 'Dad's Favourite'**
**Height** *10cm (4in).*
**Spread** *20cm (8in).*
**Flowering time** *Early to midsummer.*
**Star qualities** *Neat mats of grey foliage topped by purple-edged flowers.*
**Other varieties** *'Hidcote' has gorgeous double flowers of rich deep red; D. alpinus 'Joan's Blood' has dark green foliage and single, deep magenta flowers; 'Little Jock', an alpine pink, has richly clove-scented pale pink flowers, the petals ruffled and fringed.*

### Lagurus ovatus (Hare's tail)
*In the wild, this pretty grass grows in sandy soil in Spain and other Mediterranean countries, flowering between mid-spring and early summer. But, in cooler climates and grown from spring-sown seed, its flowering will be later. The stems may grow to 50cm (20in) but are generally shorter, each tipped with the rounded, softly hairy heads that give the grass its common name. It dries well. For the best results, pick it before the heads are fully mature.*

### Aquilegia 'Hensol Harebell'
*One of the few rules in gardening is that you can never have too many aquilegias. The foliage, greyish, slightly glaucous, is beautiful in itself and furnishes the ground from early spring. Aquilegias with long spurs floating back from the frilly cups are slightly more difficult to keep than short-spurred types. In this short-spurred cultivar, the flowers are a gorgeous soft blue on stems up to 75cm (30in). It was raised in the early 1900s by Mrs Kennedy at Mossdale, Castle Douglas, in Scotland.*

*Dianthus 'Dad's Favourite'* ▷

# Digitalis purpurea Excelsior Group *with*
# Ferula communis *and* Matteuccia struthiopteris

The common foxglove is a biennial, producing a fat rosette of leaves the first year and shooting up to flower in the second. Like other biennials, plants will self-seed profusely once established. Gardeners should welcome this profligacy, for foxgloves often have better ideas than we do about where they look best. They certainly have a clearer understanding of their own requirements in terms of shade, soil and general sustenance. But self-seeders also change the emphasis of a garden. You may have started off your foxgloves in a shady corner with ferns and giant fennel for company. But the following year you may find seedlings bouncing up between thalictrums and hostas in an entirely different part of the garden, where they will look just as good as in the place you planned for them. If you allow selected strains such as 'Sutton's Apricot' and Excelsior to seed, they gradually drift back towards the wild purple type. When the specials have disappeared, it is time to sow new seed. Unlike purple foxgloves, pale-flowered seedlings show no purple staining on leaf or stem.

### Digitalis purpurea Excelsior Group (Foxglove)

**Height** *1–2m (3–6ft).*
**Spread** *60cm (24in).*
**Flowering time** *Early summer.*
**Star qualities** *Tall, elegant spikes of flower, excellent in dappled shade. Excelsior Group plants hold their flowers out from the stem, so that you can more easily see into their spotted interiors.*
**Other varieties** D. purpurea *f.* albiflora *is the white-flowered form of the common foxglove;* 'Sutton's Apricot' *has exquisite apricot-pink flowers.*

### Ferula communis (Giant fennel)

*This is a completely different animal to the edible fennel (Foeniculum vulgare). Its main use is as a foliage plant, for though the flowering stem is dramatically vast – up to 5m (15ft) – the plant usually dies after flowering. But while building up for several years to this apocalyptic last act, it produces fountains of fresh foliage very early in the year. The green is of an unnatural brilliance, and the foliage is even more dense and feathery than its edible cousin's.*

### Matteuccia struthiopteris (Shuttlecock fern)

*These ferns erupt gently in spring to make elegant vase-shaped specimens, upright and bright, light green until autumn frosts change them to tones of yellow. They are supremely graceful and not difficult if you can provide a home that is moist but not waterlogged, perhaps in the dappled shade under trees. They are at their most beautiful when just emerging, each frond curled like a bishop's crozier.*

*Digitalis purpurea* Excelsior Group ▷

# Eryngium giganteum *with* Pelargonium 'Lady Plymouth' *and* Echeveria elegans

You need a hot, sunny, dry position for these plants, all of which have the bleached-out look of creatures used to desert conditions. It is a group to be planted mostly for form and contrasts of foliage. The fine sea holly will be the dominant feature, but it is a biennial. Be prepared, by having some young plants in reserve to stop up gaps. But it is also a vigorous self-seeder, so after a while, equilibrium will be achieved and plantings will renew themselves without your guidance. The skeletal plants dry well, but they will also stand in the garden into autumn and early winter, before birds finally pick the domed seedheads to pieces. Both the pelargonium and the echeveria are greenhouse plants, and they can only be set out in the garden when all danger of frost has passed. In temperate climates, this usually means late spring. They will then get better and better until you start to worry about frost again in early autumn and whisk them back under cover. So this is an ephemeral planting, but allows plenty of scope for change and renewal. You might experiment with aeoniums instead of echeverias, or use a heavier pelargonium, such as *P.* 'Chocolate Peppermint' with thick, felted, peppermint-scented leaves.

### *Eryngium giganteum* (Miss Willmott's ghost)

**Height** *90cm (36in).*
**Spread** *30cm (12in).*
**Flowering time** *Mid- to late summer.*
**Star qualities** *Spiny, stiff habit, which gives architectural structure to a plant group. Steely blue-grey bracts surround flowers domed like teasels. Long lasting.*
**Other varieties** E. alpinum, *with finely cut blue bracts;* E. x oliverianum, *which has thin, linear bracts of purplish silver;* E. x tripartitum, *which has relatively inconspicuous bracts and neat rounded heads of flower on a plant of open, branching habit.*

### *Pelargonium* 'Lady Plymouth'

*Scented-leaved geraniums such as this are grown more for their foliage than their flowers. 'Lady Plymouth' has finely cut leaves with silver margins. When you touch them, they release pungent waves of eucalyptus. It grows 30–40cm (12–16in) tall. The inconspicuous lavender-pink flowers are borne from mid- to late summer. It is not hardy and in areas of frost needs to be brought under cover for winter.*

### *Echeveria elegans*

*Succulent fat echeverias look as though they have been made of wax, each leaf perfectly placed to make a symmetrical rosette, which spreads gently with age. They are slow starters, but by the end of summer plump themselves up at an astonishing rate. They are not hardy, but bring an unusual, exotic air to a plant group.*

*Eryngium giganteum*

# Eschscholzia californica *with* Salvia sclarea var. sclarea *and* Calendula officinalis 'Art Shades'

For instant effect, you can scarcely beat annuals such as the California poppy (*Eschscholzia*) and the English pot marigold (*Calendula*). You simply scatter the seed (they grow particularly well through gravel) and wait. Only on very sticky, lumpy ground may they struggle to germinate. So for new gardeners, or gardeners with hot, dry spots that they can't think what to do with, or those who are gardening on borrowed ground where more permanent planting may be inappropriate, they are unbeatable. In this scheme, the brilliant orange and yellow shades of the annuals are set against the more sombre grey green of Vatican sage (*Salvia sclarea*). If you want more finesse in the colour scheme, use an eschscholzia such as 'Thai Silk', with flowers in cream and pink. 'Rose Chiffon' is even more elegant, with ruffled double flowers of deep rose. Each has a rich yellow eye. When you are planting, set the sage in place first, so you do not disturb seed or seedlings with subsequent excavations.

### Eschscholzia californica (California poppy)

**Height** *20–25cm (8–10in).*
**Spread** *15cm (6in).*
**Flowering time** *Mid- to late summer.*
**Star qualities** *Finely cut blue-green foliage. Pyramid-shaped buds burst open to reveal silky poppy flowers in a dazzling array of colours: red, pink and orange, tinted with bronze.*
**Other varieties** *'Ballerina' has fluted semi-double flowers; 'Cherry Ripe' is an elegant single red; 'Alba' has chaste creamy-white flowers; 'Apricot Flambeau' is a showy apricot double.*

### Salvia sclarea var. sclarea (Vatican sage)

*The habit of this sage is usually biennial. In the first year it produces rosettes of grey-green leaves up to 23cm (9in) long, toothed and wrinkled. From late spring to summer of the following year, it sends up pinkish many-branched stems bearing dry, papery, hooded flowers of pinkish white. It smells horrible, but provides an excellent buffer between other more brightly coloured companions.*

### Calendula officinalis 'Art Shades' (Pot marigold)

*Calendula's proper name comes from the Latin word* calendae, *the first day of the month, and is a tribute to the long flowering period of this common cottage garden flower. 'Art Shades' is a mixture blended for aesthetes in apricot, orange and cream, all with soft brown eyes. They are charming and easy annuals, flowering best in sun. Regular deadheading will prolong the display. Sow the seed where it is to flower, covering it lightly with soil. Thin out the seedlings as they develop.*

*Eschscholzia californica* ▷

# Geranium psilostemon *with* Fritillaria meleagris *and* Pulmonaria 'Lewis Palmer'

The geranium and the pulmonaria both provide excellent ground cover. The term is often used rather despairingly as though it were a last resort, like linoleum in the bathroom. Well used, ground-cover plants are among the most interesting of garden plants. They need not be baldly utilitarian, but can be knitted into groups of different colours and textures that ebb and flow through the seasons to give different effects at different times of the year. When the pulmonaria is flowering full pelt in early spring, the geranium will only just be thinking about pushing its lipstick buds above ground. But by midsummer, the pulmonaria will be all leaf while the geranium has sparked into show-stopping flower. Among the clumps of pulmonaria and geranium, use quantities of little fritillaries, not five or 10 in a group, but 20 or 30. They are one of the great joys of spring and provide as pleasant a way to bankrupt yourself as any other – so much better for your liver than alcohol.

## Geranium psilostemon
**Height** *60–120cm (24–48in).*
**Spread** *60cm (24in).*
**Flowering time** *Early to late summer.*
**Star qualities** *Generous, ground-covering foliage, a good foil for other plants. Eye-catching, tall stems of long-lasting magenta flowers.*
**Other varieties** *'Ann Folkard', a scrambler rather than a clumper, has flowers of a similar style and colour; much smaller G. cinereum 'Ballerina', with purplish-red flowers, is useful where space is limited.*

## Fritillaria meleagris (Snake's head fritillary)
*Although now rare in the wild, these fritillaries are not at all difficult to establish in the garden. They do not like to be chivvied; you just have to wait while they decide whether they like you or not. If they do, they will flower in mid-spring in their strange angular, spotted way. The flowers are chequerboards of purple and white, some flowers are white, tinged with green. The leaves are thin and grassy and the whole plant has a kind of fragile sadness that is very touching.*

## Pulmonaria 'Lewis Palmer' (Lungwort)
*In early spring, pulmonarias concentrate on producing their flowers, which in varieties such as 'Lewis Palmer' drift indeterminately from pink to mid-blue. Later, the plants turn their attention to their leaves, and these, large, hairy and mottled with silver, provide excellent ground cover during the summer. In this way, the variegated pulmonarias are much better value than types such as 'Munstead Blue' which have coarse green leaves.*

*Geranium psilostemon*

# Helenium 'Moerheim Beauty' *with* Euphorbia griffithii 'Dixter' *and* Coreopsis tinctoria

Bright yellow daisies are an essential feature of a late summer garden. They are also favourite components in the new style of "prairie planting", in which huge swathes of perennials are planted in interlocking groups and grown with minimal intervention on the part of the gardener. The style originated in the public parks of Germany and for the full effect, you need plenty of space. Prairie plants of North America, such as the helenium and the coreopsis, are of course ideal for this kind of treatment and blaze out together in late summer with complementary daisy flowers of mahogany and yellow. The inner disc of the coreopsis flower matches the rich brownish red of 'Moerheim Beauty'. The spurge (*Euphorbia*) flowers much earlier, in late spring and early summer, but its brick-coloured foliage will add its own strong contribution to the later sunburned colours of the daisies. If you do not want the bother of raising the coreopsis from seed, use a perennial rudbeckia instead.

*Helenium* 'Moerheim Beauty'
**Height** *90cm (36in).*
**Spread** *60cm (24in).*
**Flowering time** *Early to late summer.*
**Star qualities** *Rich copper-red flowers, the petals swept back from the central dark cone. Sturdy habit of growth.*
**Other varieties** *'Baudirektor Linne' is taller, with velvety, brownish-red flowers; 'Bruno' has a markedly upright habit with flowers of brownish red around a darker centre; 'Septemberfuchs' is later flowering and has brownish flowers, streaked with yellow.*

### *Euphorbia griffithii* 'Dixter'

*The great gardener Christopher Lloyd picked out this seedling from a batch growing at Washfield Nursery, near his home in Sussex. The foliage is much redder in this type than in the more common species, and provides a suitably hot setting for the flowers which are brick coloured. 'Fireglow' has the same orange-red flowers, but set against green foliage.*

### *Coreopsis tinctoria*

*This is an annual tickseed, native to North America. It has yellow daisy flowers marked at the base of the petals with a brownish red. The central discs are darker still. It grows to about 1.2m (4ft), so will hold its own against the helenium. The flowers are held on stiff, branching stems and do not usually need staking.*

*Helenium* 'Moerheim Beauty' ▷

# Hemerocallis citrina *with* Nicotiana sylvestris *and* Lupinus 'Polar Princess'

Some gardeners, working in offices a long way from their homes, see rather more of their gardens in the evening than they do during daytime. This is a group for them. Both the day lily (*Hemerocallis*) and tobacco flower (*Nicotiana*) perform more dramatically in the evening than they do at any other time of the day. They smell most strongly then, too. And that is another strength of this trio – scent. All three plants have it, the tobacco flower most outrageously, the lupin most fleetingly. Although the day lily does not start flowering until midsummer, its foliage will be furnishing the ground from early spring – bright and lush. The lupin's foliage is also excellent, a darker more sombre green and a completely different shape. But the two will flower together, with the superb *Nicotiana sylvestris* coming on later in the season.

### Hemerocallis citrina (Day lily)

**Height** *1.2m (4ft).*
**Spread** *75cm (30in).*
**Flowering time** *Midsummer.*
**Star qualities** *Bright, fresh foliage, very early into growth. Fragrant greenish-yellow flowers, which open in the evening. They are held well above the foliage.*
**Other varieties** *'Cartwheels' has yellow-gold flowers; 'Corky' grows to only 70cm (28in) with yellow flowers, darker on the reverse; 'Golden Chimes' has golden-yellow flowers opening from reddish-brown buds; 'Green Flutter' has ruffled yellow petals, green at the throat.*

### Nicotiana sylvestris (Tobacco plant)

*In rich, well-drained soil, these are easy plants, wonderfully scented, particularly in the evening. Plants are best raised from seed, in the same way as the tobacco flowers used for bedding, but this type may develop as a short-lived perennial. A well-grown plant will easily reach 1.5m (5ft), producing at the top of its stem a long succession of trumpet flowers, opening from long, narrow tubes.*

### Lupinus 'Polar Princess'

*Most garden lupins derive from the blue-flowered American species* Lupinus polyphyllus. *The first "break" was a strawberry-red lupin; subsequently breeders went on to produce a wide range of varieties, pale yellow, orange-yellow, mauve, including some fancy bicolours. 'Polar Princess' is a chaste white, producing spikes up to 90cm (36in) tall in early and midsummer.*

*Hemerocallis citrina* ▷

# Hosta 'Krossa Regal' *with* Primula florindae *and* Polygonatum falcatum 'Variegatum'

Cool, damp soil suits all three of these plants, none of which will be crying out for sun. To get the best effect from the foliage of the hosta and the Solomon's seal (*Polygonatum*), the ground needs to be rich in humus too. If you can provide all these conditions, this group may well draw you back more often than any other plants in the garden. It is a cool combination, because even the yellow of the primula is a sharp, frosty yellow, muted by the downy meal that covers its flowerheads. The hosta is one of the best of this huge family because the leaves, neither too big, nor too wide, are carried well above the ground, swelling out from strong stems to make pewter-coloured vases. The solidity of the hosta foliage is offset by the more delicate construction of the Solomon's seal, set with tiny hanging bells. Watch for the caterpillar-like larvae of the sawfly, which in early summer can strip Solomon's seal to a skeleton. The plain green-leaved variety is just as good as the variegated one.

### *Hosta* 'Krossa Regal'

**Height** *70cm (28in).*
**Spread** *75cm (30in).*
**Flowering time** *Summer.*
**Star qualities** *Large, glaucous, bluish-green leaves, held well above the ground on long stalks. Elegant sheaves of pale lilac flowers.*
**Other varieties** *'Blue Angel' has bigger leaves and white flowers; 'Frances Williams' is a subtle bicolour, blue-green centres to yellow-green-edged leaves. To accentuate the yellow in this group, use a golden-leaved cultivar such as 'Wind River Gold' or 'Zounds'.*

### *Primula florindae* (Giant cowslip)

*One of the latest of the primulas to bloom, bearing in summer drooping heads of acid yellow flowers, sometimes as many as 40 on a single stem. The petals are powdered with white meal. It is powerful enough to suppress annual weeds with its big, meaty clumps of leaves. Its home is Tibet, where it grows in marshy ground and along the banks of streams. Give it damp ground. It is deliciously scented.*

### *Polygonatum falcatum* 'Variegatum' (Variegated Solomon's seal)

*An easy-going woodland plant which will do without sun. It has an elegant habit of growth, the stems thrusting through the ground in mid-spring and bearing, by late spring, creamy-white flowers, which hang all along the stems. In this form, the leaves, which grow in pairs along the stems, are thinly edged with white. In cool, humus-rich soil, Solomon's seal spreads quickly by underground rhizomes.*

*Hosta* 'Krossa Regal'

# Lilium regale *with* Salvia patens 'Cambridge Blue' *and* Nicotiana x sanderae

Since lilies hate to be disturbed, it is worth spending time in getting their home right before you plant them. Plenty of humus, combined with excellent drainage, gives the best results. *Lilium regale* is one of the best known of all lilies, because, compared with other white lilies such as the Madonna lily or Japanese lilies of the *L. auratum* type, it is an accommodating thing. Plant the scaly bulbs in either autumn or spring and mulch them annually in spring with leaf-mould or very well-rotted compost. Underground slugs are the lilies' worst enemy. Set the bulbs on sharp gritty sand when you plant them, and surround them with more grit as you cover them up. Arrange to have this group by a seat in the garden, so that in the evening you can swim in the scent. The cocktail of lily and tobacco flower will be far more intoxicating than wine. Avoid using tobacco flowers with no scent. Breeders produce them, heaven knows why, and the lack of scent is often allied to a lack of stature. Horrid.

### Lilium regale
**Height** *90cm (36in).*
**Spread** *30cm (12in).*
**Flowering time** *Midsummer.*
**Star qualities** *Beautifully scented trumpets, white, but washed over on the backs of the petals with purplish brown. Easy to grow in most soils except very alkaline ones.*
**Other varieties** *Swing the group into pink mode by using a lily such as 'Barbara North', with scented, turkscap flowers; the white Madonna lily,* L. candidum, *is beautiful but not so easy to grow as* L. regale.

### Nicotiana x sanderae (Tobacco plant)
*This group of plants is named after Jan Nicot, an ambassador who, in the 16th century, introduced tobacco into France. There are many different kinds. 'Fragrant Cloud' is a strong-growing variety, reaching 90cm (36in), with beautifully scented white flowers. 'Sensation Mixed' is equally tall and well scented but has flowers in a mixed range of colours. The best scent comes from white or green flowers, but it is much stronger in the evening than it is during the day.*

### Salvia patens 'Cambridge Blue'
*If it is not knocked back by frost, this salvia eventually makes a fleshy underground tuber like a dahlia's, though it is nothing like as vigorous in growth. Foliage is mid-green and, in this variety, the beaky flowers are pale sky-blue, but a piercing blue in the standard species. As with most salvias, there is a greater proportion of leaf to flower than one would wish.*

*Lilium regale*

# Nepeta 'Six Hills Giant' *with* Zinnia Allsorts *and* Nicotiana langsdorffii

There is no better way to bring change and pace to a summer garden than by using annuals, which reach their flowering peak when other, earlier summer plants are beginning to look tired and dowdy. This group includes two annuals, one recessive and curious, the other wildly extrovert and sexy. Though zinnias are Mexican by nature, they will put up with cooler, wetter climates, but they become much leafier as a result. The catmint, a perennial, provides bulk and a quiet, undemanding backdrop against which the annual fireworks can explode. Cut clumps of catmint back hard after the first flowering to encourage a later repeat performance. In cold areas, leave the withered stems for protection against winter cold. The catmint, like the annual flowers which accompany it in this group, prefers full sun and well-drained soil. If you want the whole scheme to be cool and recessive, use a different zinnia. Both 'Green Envy' and 'Envy Double' echo the cool, minty quality of *N. langsdorffii*.

**Nepeta 'Six Hills Giant' (Catmint)**
**Height** *90cm (36in).*
**Spread** *60cm (24in).*
**Flowering time** *Summer.*
**Star qualities** *A very vigorous catmint, which produces masses of aromatic grey-green foliage, the leaves small, matt and crinkled. Against this soft background, greyish-blue spikes of flower are presented over a long season in summer.*
**Other varieties** N. sibirica *'Souvenir d'André Chaudron' is shorter, but each individual flower is bigger than the norm.*

### *Zinnia* Allsorts
*Mixtures, such as this assortment of zinnias, do not generally give the best effect in a garden. This one is different. It contains a wide range of types and each one is a wonder. Some flowers are single, in weird psychedelic combinations of pink and orange, others are hugely double with ruffled centres between splayed outer petals. Pink, red, orange and yellow predominate, though there is a startling pale green too.*

### *Nicotiana langsdorffii* (Tobacco plant)
*A native of Brazil with tall sticky stems often more than 1m (3ft) high. The flowers are small but enchantingly arranged on the wide branching stems. Each one has a long thin neck which flares at the end into a rounded bell shape. This annual is in no way a showy plant, but it is an intriguing one. If you want something noisier, then grow the cultivar 'Lime Green'.*

# Nigella damascena 'Miss Jekyll' *with*
# Stachys byzantina *and* Viola 'Belmont Blue'

Love-in-a-mist (*Nigella*) was introduced from Damascus more than 400 years ago and has remained a popular cottage garden flower ever since. The swollen seedpods are a great feature when the display of flowers comes to an end. They can be cut, dried and used in decorations inside. In this group, it will be best to get the two low-growing perennials, the stachys and the viola, established before you introduce the nigella, which is an annual, growing from fresh seed each year. Prepare the seedbed carefully, in between the other plants, breaking down any intractable lumps of soil. Sow the seed thinly in mid-spring and cover with a fine scattering of soil. If necessary, thin the seedlings as they emerge, to allow each to develop properly. In suitable soils, the plants will self-seed, saving you the bother of replacing them each year. If self-seeding doesn't happen, seize the opportunity to try something different – cornflowers perhaps, or intriguing salpigossis, with dark trumpet flowers veined in contrasting tones.

### Nigella damascena 'Miss Jekyll' (Love-in-a-mist)
**Height** *45cm (18in).*
**Spread** *23cm (9in).*
**Flowering time** *Summer.*
**Star qualities** *Sky-blue flowers surrounded by a ruff of finely divided tendrils. An annual, but generally self-seeds profusely. Fine, filigree foliage and seedheads like small balloons. They dry well.*
**Other varieties** *N. hispanica is a fine dark blue species, the centre of each flower a showy wine colour. Taller and wider spreading than N. damascena.*

### Stachys byzantina (Lambs' ears)
*Although it can look bedraggled in winter or after heavy summer rain, this is an excellent plant. It prefers well-drained soil for, like most of the greys, it will rot away if it is too damp. It needs picking over regularly so that the yellowing and withered leaves do not spoil the overall effect. 'Silver Carpet' is a good non-flowering form of this well-known ground coverer.*

### Viola 'Belmont Blue'
*The violas are a vast family, embracing the large monkey-faced pansies as well as tiny wildlings such as V. odorata. 'Belmont Blue' (syn. 'Boughton Blue') is a good clear blue and, like so many of this tribe, profligate with its flowers. To keep up their superhuman display, violas need feeding as well as regular deadheading. If plants get leggy, cut the stems back to a joint close to the base. Shear back the entire plant in late summer.*

*Nigella damascena*
'Miss Jekyll'

# Phlox carolina 'Miss Lingard' *with* Petunia 'Prime Time White' *and* Penstemon 'Apple Blossom'

The colours here are porcelain china: pale and pure. But there is great potential for change. If you substituted the mauve-blue penstemon 'Alice Hindley' for the pink and white 'Apple Blossom' and introduced a rich purplish-blue petunia instead of the white one, you would shift the group into much more saturated mode. But not everyone likes dark, rich colours and this group is for them. It is safe and will go with anything that happens to impinge on it. Phloxes like hefty meals, so in autumn, when you have cleared away the remains of the petunias, you should mulch the cut-down phloxes with well-rotted manure or compost. The clumps will need splitting and replanting every few years. Do this in autumn or spring. Get rid of all the woody growth and replant only the vigorous new pieces growing round the sides of the clump.

### Phlox carolina 'Miss Lingard'

**Height** *1.2m (4ft).*
**Spread** *45cm (18in).*
**Flowering time** *Summer.*
**Star qualities** *Dense heads of flower that are washing-powder white. Strong constitution. Gives a charming, cottage-garden air to any group.*
**Other varieties** P. paniculata *'Fujiyama' is a distinctive variety with cylindrical heads of white flowers on sturdy stems and 'White Admiral' has shapely heads of equally pure white.*

### Petunia 'Prime Time White'

*Petunias come from South America and have been eagerly seized on by plant breeders who have produced some hideous mixtures of colours. This single white is charming. Though not as showy as the double kinds, singles are better equipped to cope with bad weather. Petunias like full sun and a light soil. Drought suits them rather well; rain is more of a problem.*

### Penstemon 'Apple Blossom'

*Some cultivars belonging to this desirable group are bigger than others. 'Apple Blossom' rarely exceeds 45–60cm (18–24in) in any direction. All are beautiful, but not reliably hardy. Damp is as big an enemy as frost and you will please this penstemon by finding it a well-drained spot in full sun. Do not cut down the stems in autumn as new shoots will be slaughtered by frost. Wait instead until spring to tidy up plants.*

*Phlox carolina*
'Miss Lingard'

# Rodgersia aesculifolia *with* Iris laevigata 'Variegata' *and* Ligularia 'The Rocket'

The iris will be the first of the flowers to bloom in this group, carrying a succession of palely perfect flowers from early summer onwards. By the time the ligularia and rodgersia come into play, from midsummer onwards, the iris will have finished. That is just as well, because its own quiet voice would be drowned by the fortissimo performance of the others, especially the ligularia which has uncompromisingly bold flowers. But even without flowers, this group will be worth looking at because all the plants have superb foliage. The hand-shaped leaves of the rodgersia are set against the more rounded outlines of the ligularia foliage. The iris provides punctuation marks, solid uprights, eye-catchingly variegated, among the other mounds. All enjoy the same damp conditions, but the rodgersia is much slower to bulk up than the ligularia. Do not let it get swamped.

### Rodgersia aesculifolia

**Height** *1.2m (4ft).*
*Spread 1m (3ft).*
**Flowering time** *Midsummer onwards.*
**Star qualities** *Superb foliage, toothed leaflets in hand-shaped clusters, like the horse chestnut which gives it its name. Strong tall panicles of flower with the texture of plush. Both pink and white forms are available.*
**Other varieties** R. pinnata *'Superba' (see p.90) has similar hand-shaped leaves, heavily burnished with purplish bronze when they first emerge in late spring;* R. podophylla *has jagged leaves and creamy flowers that appear from mid- to late summer.*

### Iris laevigata 'Variegata'

*Not so tall as the yellow flag iris (I. pseudacorus, see p.108), this iris has striking foliage, growing up to 45cm (18in) and striped in soft cream and pale green. This is a variegation that murmurs rather than shouts, and is wonderful with the lavender-blue flowers that come out in summer. It needs moist soil and will even grow happily with its feet dangling in water.*

### Ligularia 'The Rocket'

*Big rounded leaves with jagged, toothed edges that grow best where the soil is moist and rich. Both the leaf stalks and the stems bearing the flowers are almost black, a dramatic foil to the brilliant orange-yellow flowerheads. These are produced over a long season from early to late summer. All the ligularias are hefty things, but among the best of all plants for bogs and pool sides.*

*Rodgersia aesculifolia* ▷

# Verbascum chaixii 'Gainsborough' *with* Campanula lactiflora 'Prichard's Variety' *and* Callistephus 'Florette Champagne'

These plants would have been as familiar in a Victorian border as they are today. They are classic components of a summer flower garden and, in the varieties chosen here, will provide a muted palette of colours, as soft and hazy as summer twilight. Both verbascum and campanula are tall and willowy in growth, the verbascum more spire-like than the campanula. That is why you need tall China asters (*Callistephus*) to go with them. This is a group for summer show, though the asters, given a calm, quiet autumn, will go on producing flowers astonishingly late in the season. But you can easily introduce spring interest by packing pale narcissi round the rosettes of the verbascum, remembering, of course, how large the leaves are likely to be when they are full grown. All this group lacks is scent. If this is a priority, substitute evening primrose (*Oenothera biennis*) for the verbascum.

### Verbascum chaixii 'Gainsborough'

**Height** *1.2m (4ft).*
**Spread** *30cm (12in).*
**Flowering time** *Early to late summer.*
**Star qualities** *Strong rosettes of wrinkled, grey-green leaves. Tall spikes of soft yellow flowers.*
**Other varieties** *'Cotswold Beauty' has flowers of buff-apricot; 'Pink Domino' has deep rose-pink flowers; 'Helen Johnson' has pinkish-brown flowers; 'Letitia' has flat flowers of a good, clear yellow.*

### Campanula lactiflora 'Prichard's Variety'

*A good-natured campanula, which will thrive anywhere – even in rough grass. It has strong stems, set at the top with big branching heads of flower, deep violet-blue in this variety. In windy, exposed positions, it may need staking, for it will easily shoot up to 1.2m (4ft). To shift the scheme into pink mode, use 'Loddon Anna', a lilac-pink that will blend easily with the soft yellow of the verbascum, the colours of sugared almonds.*

### Callistephus 'Florette Champagne'

*Annual asters, such as this, are outrageously wonderful flowers, provided they are not rained on too much. They are asters that think they are chrysanthemums and this one has extraordinary, spidery petals whirling round madly in an effort to catch one another. The colour is a soft creamy pink, chosen to blend with the creamy yellow of the verbascum. For a stronger contrast, choose more traditional mixes of purple and blue.*

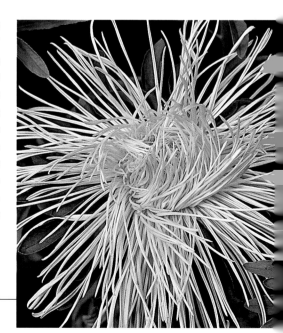

*Verbascum chaixii*
'Gainsborough'

WHAT WOULD YOUR STAR PLANT BE in this heady season as late summer drifts into autumn? With frost hovering in the wings, we garden now with a particular kind of recklessness. Each day might be the last that we can gaze on a tumble of brilliant nasturtiums lolloping along a border. Each fresh bud that appears

# into autumn

seems a hostage to fortune. Would your star plant perhaps be a dahlia? If you've always been frightened of dahlias, acclimatize yourself gradually by growing a strain of the fine species *D. coccinea* with single, chalky red flowers, held on wide airy stems. The whole plant is less hefty and congested than a hybrid. Or perhaps, as your favourite, you might choose *Canna* x *ehemanii*, with vast, paddle-shaped leaves that unfurl gradually from high summer.

### Fan the flames
*Like tongues of fire, the orange and yellow spikes of a red hot poker* (Kniphofia rooperi) *lick round the dying heads of a cardoon* (Cynara cardunculus). *Between them are plumes of a relatively compact pampas grass,* Cortaderia selloana *'Pumila'.*

## Triumphal cannas

*Cannas, such as lustrous 'Durban', are not for faint-hearted gardeners. Their vast painted leaves dominate any company they happen to be in. The dark red spike of Lobelia 'Dark Crusader' on the right scarcely makes an impression, though the heleniums behind make sure they are noticed by jostling together in a big crowd.*

The flowers come later, held in elegant, drooping panicles, unlike most other cannas which flower on stiff, upright spikes. Both are late starting into growth, so to get the most out of your garden, you might need to arrange an ephemeral display of spring bulbs to cover the ground while these two get going. In cold areas, both will have been lifted from the ground and stored under cover for winter. In milder areas, the tubers may overwinter in the ground, under an eiderdown of dry leaves.

Both dahlias and cannas are very leafy, but when their flowers emerge, they are uncompromising in colour. If you are planting them with companions that flower at the same time, think deep red, deep blue, purple, magenta, pink, cream and buff. All those shades will blend happily with them. But, given the fact that both dahlia and canna are late starters, you may choose instead a plant that peaks at an entirely different season and reach perhaps for the fine old double peony *P. officinalis* 'Rubra Plena'.

Or you could build on the leafy theme, aiming for a subtropical, almost jungly look with plumes of royal fern (*Osmunda regalis*), rough hands of rodgersia with buff flowers, the great crinkled cabbage leaves of crambe, scimitar-shaped fans of crinum, whose trumpet flowers will join those of the dahlia and canna in late summer, or fronds of *Geranium palmatum*.

Purple-leaved bugbane (*Cimicifuga simplex* Atropurpurea Group) is another possibility, a beautiful thing which will grow up to 1.2m (4ft), the leaves elegantly lobed and cut. It flowers in late autumn, with long, thin creamy spikes, so, like the crinum, coincides with the dahlia and the canna. Though the crinum's flowers are far showier, the bugbane has the advantage of foliage, deep, saturated in colour and well made enough to provide a feature on its own earlier in the season.

Purply-bronze, too, is the sedum 'Lynda et Rodney' which is one of the tall growing kinds, a cultivar of *Sedum telephium*, but not so dark and beefy as *S. telephium* 'Atropurpureum'. Like bugbanes, the sedums are useful performers at a time when most of the garden is winding down. If you wanted more lightness and movement in the group, you might choose a grass such as *Pennisetum macrourum*, a clumping, evergreen plant which has flower spikelets like caterpillars hanging off the end of its stems in autumn. They start pale creamy green and turn purple and brown as they age. The grass would have the advantage of leavening the heavier foliage of dahlia or canna, especially the canna. Purple coneflowers (*Echinacea purpurea*), would be another possibility, though the foliage is coarse, perhaps too coarse to put with canna or dahlia.

If you want to keep your options open, you might choose less permanent plantings. You could join up clumps of sweet William with groups of the dark-flowered snapdragon 'Purple King', not one of the hideous dwarfed varieties, but a sensible snapdragon, about 45cm (18in) in height. Sometimes, both sweet Williams and snapdragons hang on as short-lived perennials and consequently come into flower much earlier than plants raised from seed. Then their flowering will not coincide with either the dahlia or the canna. But if you remember to cut off the main spike of a snapdragon after it has flowered, lesser spikelets will flower on much later into autumn. 'Corona Mixed', undwarfed at 50cm (20in), is a strong-growing strain (though sprawling by nature) and flowers in a good mix of colours. For a dark-leaved, deep red snapdragon to put alongside *Canna* x *ehemanii* and the elegant grass *Pennisetum macrourum*, try 'Black Prince'.

*Osmunda regalis*, p.90
*Rodgersia aesculifolia*, p.174, and *R. pinnata* 'Superba', p.90
*Crambe cordifolia*, p.74
*Geranium palmatum*, p.82
*Cimicifuga simplex* 'Brunette', p.200

*Canna* x *ehemanii*, p.198

*Cerinthe major*
'Purpurascens', p.144

*Petunia* 'Purple Wave', p.94

Cerinthe is another useful plant to keep in reserve as a filler. You might also use some small-flowered, weather-resistant petunias or the wide-spreading petunias often called Surfinias. There is an excellent one called 'Purple Wave'. The plants are phenomenal flowerers, most often used in containers, but they are good on the flat too.

Dramatic late summer effects can be created in the garden using nothing but annuals, exploiting their capacity to flower late and encouraging them to take over from earlier-flowering perennials. There is a huge range of colours available from annual flowers. That is a blessing, of course, but it also calls for forethought on the part of the gardener. The best effects will

## *Your garden can look as rich and profligate in late summer and autumn as it does in late spring.*

arise from having a particular colour scheme in mind. It might be yellow, which can blaze away in the company of the oranges and bronzes that come from rudbeckias and heleniums. Teamed with lime green and white, yellow will become cooler, more classical. Either combination could contain enormous sunflowers, with heads big enough to knock you out, should they happen to fall your way.

*Cosmos bipinnatus* 'Sonata White', p.148

If you go for a cool effect, lime-green nicotiana will be one of your stalwarts, growing at its proper height, rather than in a dwarfed state. White cosmos will be another, the clean simple flowers set against surprisingly good foliage. There are not many annuals noted for their leaves. Both these flowers are easy to raise from seed and go together well, the tobacco flower's stodgy foliage relieved by the featheriness of the other. Try them with tall and acid yellow African marigolds, then lace the whole lot together with creeping tendrils of lime-green helichrysum. Alternatively, the white in this kind of scheme might come from frilly petunias and snapdragons, planted again with the lime-green nicotianas and a foreground of *Sanvitalia procumbens*. This is a low-growing daisy-ish sort of plant, small single yellow flowers with prominent black centres.

Or you could try grey helichrysum instead of the lime-green one, letting it bob up among yellow snapdragons and seed-raised bedding dahlias. The

'Redskin' mixture produces double dahlias, set against lustrous bronze foliage. For a change, substitute English marigolds instead of the African and French kinds. Or underplant tall yellow and white zinnias with alyssum and *Nierembergia* 'Mont Blanc'. Most of these combinations stick to the same yellow, lime-green and white theme, but each will give subtly different blends either side of the same path: mirror planting, but slewed enough to be interesting.

For a completely different, much more formal effect (though still using the same palette of colours), divide up a rectangular bed into a trellis design with bands of clipped grey santolina, then fill the shapes made by the santolina with lime-green coleus (*Solenostemon*). Set tall standards of Paris daisies (*Argyranthemum foeniculaceum*), with grey foliage and white daisy flowers, at the outer corners of the trellis diamonds. Plants such as coleus, which we think of as conservatory or house plants, are now being used outside by experimentally-minded gardeners. Spider plants too, and the polka dot plant, *Hypoestes phyllostachya*, which looks good combined

## Saturation point
*Not all dahlias are heavy-weights. Vermilion red 'Tally Ho' has easy-to-manage single flowers, well displayed against foliage that is almost black. Its partner is the dark-leaved* Sedum telephium *'Atropurpureum'.*

with penstemons and regular eruptions of airy *Gillenia trifolata*. This is a perennial that looks as if it might be a bulb. In the second half of summer it sends up flowering stems which explode into a branching series of small white flowers, the calyces a marked reddish brown. It is a most elegant plant and without it, the penstemon and polka dot brigade might look too congested. Gillenia grows about a metre (3ft) tall and does not seem fussy about soil or position. It is such a relief to know that some plants at least are not going to throw histrionic tantrums at critical moments.

## SEASON OF THE SUNFLOWER

Sunflowers could easily be the stars of a quick-fix garden to peak late in the season, when they could rise out of a sea of nasturtiums and lord it over dahlias in the same range of colours. They are at their best in late summer. Over the last few years they've become as sexy as the rarest salvia ever was. But so much easier. Nor do they take themselves as seriously. Nothing is as effective at lightening the urban jungle. They grow *fast*. Sow them in late spring, setting each seed into a 7cm (3in) pot. Watered well, then wrapped in clingfilm, the pots should need no attention until the seedlings poke through. The plants can go outside in late spring when all danger of frost has passed. Sunflowers generally take four months to start flowering from seed. If you sow early, they will peak early. 'Ruby Sunset' has lovely mahogany petals set around dark centres. Try it with cannas and among tall stands of miscanthus or stipa.

Because sunflowers have become so deeply fashionable as cut flowers, the bonus for gardeners is that there are now masses of different kinds to choose from. 'Moonwalker', for instance, is a branching type about 1.2m (4ft) tall with pale yellow flowers. 'Full Sun' is a more traditional golden yellow type, and 'Gold and Silver' has yellow flowers above soft velvet leaves of a silvery grey-green.

Colours range upwards and downwards from the standard bright yellow to include a pale ivory and a deep, rich mahogany. Sunflowers have been planted in English cottage gardens for so long they seem part of the scenery, but, like so many English garden flowers, they are in fact foreigners. Brought over from America in the sixteenth century, English gardeners first learned about them in *Joyfull Newes out of the Newe Founde Worlde*, translated in 1577 by the super-optimist John Frampton. "It casteth out the greatest flowers," he wrote, "and the moste perticulars that ever

*Helianthus* 'Gold and Silver', p.204

## *There is no quicker way to change the look of a garden than by planting annuals.*

hath been seen, for it is greater than a great Platter or Dishe, the which hath divers coulers... It showeth marveilous faire in Gardines."

From the same part of the world at about the same time came the nasturtium, which you can also start off in pots for a late summer garden. 'Jewel of Africa' has trailing shoots of marbled foliage. 'Empress of India' is much bushier with steely blue-green leaves and deep, luscious red flowers. Nasturtiums are a gamble. Sometimes they get choked with blackfly, but unmolested, they quickly spread to make a weed-suppressing mat of colour under other plants. They may even try to climb up the sunflowers' stems. The sunflowers are strong enough to take on such assaults.

*Tropaeolum majus* 'Jewel of Africa', p.74; *T. majus* 'Empress of India', p.146

### EXPLOITING ANNUALS

Annual flowers provide the icing on the cake of the garden. You can't survive for long on them alone. But there isn't any reason to deny yourself the pleasure of having them alongside other more sustaining ingredients. And though your cake recipe may stay roughly the same each year, you can experiment with different trimmings. There is no quicker way to change the look of a garden than by planting annuals; not the same ones each year, but different plants in different colours, set in different places. Some peak in high summer and have run out by late summer, but many are slower to get into top gear and are at their best as summer drifts through into autumn.

Any garden centre can supply a standard palette of annuals: French marigolds, lobelias, geraniums, petunias, busy Lizzies. But after you have run through all those permutations (remembering that these are standards because they are reliable, tough survivors) any gardener with an ounce of curiosity wants to experiment with plants that the garden centre does not provide. You need to be aware, though, that it is not a seed merchant's business to tell you how difficult certain things are to grow well. In the pages of their catalogues, all is sweetness and light. Glorious, choice, exquisite, outstanding, lovely, showy and distinctive are the words you'll find again and again. Beware, particularly, of "distinctive". It is a sign of desperation on the seed merchant's part.

Increasingly, too, you find "dwarf" put forward as a virtue. Why? Why is it a good thing to stick eleven dwarf plants into a space that five decent-sized ones could occupy more elegantly? As we are not getting any closer to the ground ourselves, dwarfing plants is a perverse trend. Let us hope it will soon come to an end. Fortunately, not all annuals respond to dwarfing. You are reasonably safe with an annual coreopsis such as *C. grandiflora* 'Early Sunrise'. The general effect is that of a dandelion, but that is not a criticism. The coreopsis's foliage does not equal the dandelion's and it does not have the wonderful seedhead. But it has bright yellow semi-double flowers, getting into gear in high summer, but peaking in late summer and autumn. Plants grow about 45cm (18in) tall. Although there are plenty of buds on each, only one flower is out at a time, so they are not showy.

Placing is important, with annuals as with any other kind of plant in the garden. It is no good raising plants if you do not then show them off to best advantage. First, you have to put the plants where they are most likely to thrive. Generally, annuals do better in the sun than shade (though that is not true of 'Non Stop' begonias or busy Lizzies). Then they need friendly neighbours that will complement them in colour and form and not overwhelm them in terms of size.

Sometimes you might make groups entirely of annuals, although generally they look best combined with more permanent features. Take a cordyline for instance – a handsome plant by any criterion. But if you pack deep purple heliotrope and deep pink ivy-leaved geraniums around its feet, it begins to look more generous (and interesting). The vanilla scent of heliotrope is reason enough to grow it, but the foliage is dramatic too: deep green with a purplish flush and the leaves furrowed by their network of veins. Like geraniums, the best kinds are perennials used as annuals, and you can keep them going by cuttings.

If you have an aversion to pink, the cordyline might be underplanted with blue *Salvia farinacea* and acid-yellow French marigolds. It might be *S. farinacea* 'Strata' which recently waltzed out of European trial grounds with a gold medal. It has spikes of blue flowers emerging from floury white calyces and grows to about 40cm (16in). "The first bicolour!" boasted the breeders. But actually, it is not as telling a plant as the older

variety 'Queen Victoria', where rich blue suffuses the stems as well as the flowers. That makes it more dramatic. Try it mixed with tall, willowy purple *Verbena bonariensis* and dark purple 'Ragged Jack' kale, which is much too handsome to bury in the vegetable patch.

Blue and yellow always work well together and you might start off with a foreground of yellow daisy-flowered bidens, which has fine, ferny foliage. Behind, you could set one of the tender blue potato-flowered solanums (it might be *S. rantonnetii*, though jagged-leaved *S. laciniatum* would be just as good). Mix these with a yellow rudbeckia. If you want an annual, go for *R. hirta* var. *pulcherrima* which makes well-branched plants, loaded with flowers. And they are tall. Hurrah! If you decide on a more permanent planting, choose one of the many excellent perennial rudbeckias, such as 'Goldsturm' which has yellow daisy flowers with dark brown cones, or 'Goldquelle' where the lemon–yellow flowers have slightly green centres. Asters come in gentler colours, the colours of sugar almonds, but provide a welcome lift in late summer planting schemes.

**The show goes on**

*Yellow daisy flowers are staple ingredients in many autumn gardens. This black-eyed Susan* (Rudbeckia fulgida) *does not start its performance as early as the* Ageratum *'Blue Horizon' with it, but continues to flower steadily until mid-autumn.*

187

Unfortunately in damp, overcast summers, they melt to make little heaps of powdery mildew wherever they have been planted.

Californian poppies, nasturtiums and pot marigolds are also reliable staples. They are all easy, cheerful flowers and you need a few stalwarts you can depend on while traitorous novelties are miffing off all around you. They are good flowers to use in mixes with vegetables too: Californian poppies with frizzy endive or lettuce, nasturtiums to make a carpet under standard gooseberries, pot marigolds to jazz up a planting of spinach. You could also try planting sunflowers among your sweet corn.

Daisy-flowered bidens is another dependable performer. If you sow seed of a strain such as 'Golden Goddess' you can raise enough plants to plant out in borders as well as fill pots, which is where they are more often used. Set them to scramble through the branches of a ceratostigma, or loll in the arms of a spring-flowering daphne. Like the snapdragon, bidens is by nature perennial, but rarely, in countries chillier than its Mexican homeland, gets the chance to settle into that comfortable habit. Without something to lean on, the plants flop, which is why they are so often used in containers. But you can use them too in the foreground of a mixed planting, where they might spill over a path or fuzz the edges of a border.

## GARDENING DANGEROUSLY

The way you approach autumn in the garden depends on your character and state of mind. You may by this stage be itching to cut everything down, clear everything away and start thinking about something else instead. Or you may want to continue gardening as vividly, joyously and dangerously as you do for the rest of the year. In which case, you will delight in the notion that you can gallop into autumn surrounded by blazing dahlias, forests of zinnias, cannas and banana palms. Instead of watching a traditional herbaceous border quietly falling apart at the seams, you can have explosions of pampas and sunflowers, eruptions of zinnias and dahlias, which by now will be at the top of their form. If you want it to, your garden can look as rich and profligate in late summer and autumn as it does in late spring. After all, there are kniphofias, such as orange-red *K. rooperi* that have not even begun to flower yet.

Try plunging pots of sweet-smelling *Gladiolus callianthus* (*syn. Acidanthera*) among coleus and pale grey succulents with leaves the shape of cows' tongues. Mix with them the tall blue flowering spikes of *Salvia farinacea* and elegant umbels of tulbaghia. Where has tulbaghia been all my life, you may ask when you first see it. It's like an allium, but lighter in build, the flowers pinkish mauve, the heads smaller than those of most alliums. Make a virtue of the fact that autumn's colours are fire colours, by planting dahlias such as the orange 'Ellen Huston', setting the blazing colour against the dark, sulky foliage of castor oil plants. Use glowing 'Orange Mullet' with the tender Bhutan ginger *Hedychium greenei*. Try the rich pink dahlia 'Pearl of Heemstede' against the velvety Mexcian salvia *S. involucrata* 'Bethellii'. If that is too pink for you, tone the group down with dark blue-flowered *Solanum rantonnetii*, the kind of thing you might normally think of using in a conservatory. Forget the conservatory. Live dangerously. Experiment with other plants such as papyrus and begonia, that you may be more used to thinking of as house plants. It is extraordinary what they can do when given their heads outside.

## VERSATILE GRASSES

Unless you have been asleep in the compost heap for the past five years, you can scarcely fail to have noticed, either, what a huge impact grasses can make in an autumn garden. There are about 9,000 species of grass in the world and it is a pity that our early conditioning with lawnmowers and hoes should lead us to think of them as enemies. There are many different kinds – miscanthus, festuca, calamagrostis and stipa – which are stars. For late summer and autumn effects, few other plants are so accommodating. When perennials begin to sag at the knees, grasses, with their elegant deportment and long-lasting seedheads, still look handsome.

Unfortunately most grasses are not yet widespread enough to have acquired common names and their proper names feel as uncomfortable in the mouth as a half-chewed dictionary. Who but the most prissy horticulturist calls *Phalaris arundinacea* anything but gardener's garters? Equally easy escape routes are needed for the rest, especially such indigestibles as arrhenatherum and hakonechloa.

Hakonechloa, a low, tussocky grass from Japan, makes clumps about 30cm (12in) across and as much high. The leaves are reasonably broad and splay out from the centre of the clump to make a half-sphere of foliage, yellow with fine green stripes. It is odd rather than beautiful, so much like a fright-wig that it is difficult to take seriously. But it makes a striking companion for purple sage and chocolate-scented *Cosmos atrosanguineus*.

*Stipa gigantea*, p.204

*Dahlia coccinea*, p.198
*Ricinus communis* 'Impala', p.198

## Winter's spell

*Frost brings many treats to an end in the garden, but initiates some splendid effects of its own. It has added a silvery veneer to the rough leaves of* Phlomis russeliana *and causes the normally upright leaves of* Melianthus major *to droop in submission. The feathery heads of* Stipa tenuissima *remain unperturbed.*

At the other end of the scale are the grasses such as *Stipa gigantea* that leap up to 2.5m (8ft) in a single season, arching like fountains as they go. These types look best planted so that they do not get too closely muddled with their neighbours, but can stand unencumbered. Nothing that we can do for them will make them more beautiful than they are themselves. We can, however, give them decent neighbours. Try clumps of the fine caterpillar-headed *Pennisetum setaceum* with the single red-flowered *Dahlia coccinea* and castor oil plants (*Ricinus*).

Grasses are generally seen to best advantage when their thin foliage is contrasted with plants that have completely different leaves, like acanthus, hostas or bergenias. Use variegated carex (not stictly a grass but a sedge), perhaps *Carex riparia* 'Variegata', behind a solid pool of low-growing

epimediums, miscanthus behind astrantia, Bowles' sedge (*Carex elata* 'Aurea') with some big, green-leaved hosta and perhaps a foreground of the bronze-leaved celandine *Ranunculus* 'Brazen Hussy'.

*Ranunculus ficaria* 'Brazen Hussy', p.74

The foxy red- and copper-toned leaves of *Carex buchananii* associate well with whipcord hebes and spiky bronze cordylines. For a Mediterranean effect, try *Stipa gigantea*, at least 2.5m (8ft) high with huge, drooping oat-like heads of seed in late summer, together with phormiums such as 'Bronze Baby' or 'Cream Delight'. Or you might choose a planting scheme that combines *S. gigantea* with orange dahlias and yellow sunflowers. The great advantage of the grasses is that they continue long after most perennials have dived underground for cover. The foliage becomes sere and dry, the seedheads fade to shades of buff and cream, but the shapes remain strongly architectural.

The stems can stand until early spring. Then they need to be cut back hard, before new growth begins. If you plant in well-prepared ground, incorporating a hefty amount of muck, the grasses will not need any more feeding. Some need restraint rather than encouragement. Gardeners' garters and the creamy-yellow-striped *Glyceria maxima* var. *variegata* are both rabid colonizers and need to be kept severely in check every autumn. Trench round the clumps with a sharp spade, as though you were digging a moat, and throw away any part of the plant that has strayed outside this *cordon sanitaire*.

Not all grasses are perennial. Annual and biennial types are easy to raise from seed and make excellent front-of-border companions for pinks or thrifts (*Armeria*) or other plants that enjoy the same sunny position and light, free-draining soil as the grasses. The quaking grass, *Briza maxima*, has particularly good seedheads like small woven lockets which tremble on thread-like stems. *Pennisetum villosum* has soft, feathery plumed heads like woolly cream caterpillars. White hare's tail, *Lagurus ovatus*, has shorter, furry heads, equally soft and graceful. This is a worthwhile plant to set between low-growing pinks and aquilegias, to take over from early De Caen anemones, or to break up patches of Swan river daisies (*Brachyscome*). The hare's tails, like perennial grasses, are at their best in late summer and autumn. In early leaf, the plants look suspiciously like weeds, but then they produce their soft furry seedheads, creamy coloured and enchanting. They are no more than 25cm (10in) high and wide, so you need plenty of them, but they are generous with their flowers. Sow seed in early spring, prick

*Lagurus ovatus*, p.150

out the seedlings into seed trays and plant them out in late spring. If you use them among pinks and aquilegias, the grass's flowering will start after the other two have finished. These annual grasses are fairly short, up to 50cm (20in), and their interest lies mostly in the seedheads. The foliage is, well, grassy.

Some of the bigger perennial grasses, such as miscanthus, take time to settle in and start flowering. But they are handsome enough to be worth using for the sake of their leaves alone. Try *Miscanthus sinensis*, which has

## Grasses' proper names feel as uncomfortable in the mouth as a half-chewed dictionary.

narrow blue-green leaves, each with a white midrib. Even better is its child 'Variegatus', the variegation a soft buff-yellow, much easier to place in a garden than 'Zebrinus', which has yellow stripes across the leaf rather than down it. The flowering plumes of *M. sinensis* 'Silberfeder' make it seem like a scaled-down pampas grass and the season is equally long. The plumes start opening at the end of summer and are still in good form by the end of the year.

Suddenly grasses are fashionable plants, which means that more and more different types are being introduced. Look for *Dactylis glomerata* 'Variegata', which grows about 60cm (24in) high. It has slender leaves edged in white and dramatic, chunky black seedheads. Try *Festuca punctoria* from Turkey. It has stiff, spiky leaves of silvery blue, no more than 15cm (6in) high. It often does rather better in a garden than the more common *Festuca glauca*, which, whenever you see it, seems either not quite out or else just past its best. And make your autumn garden shine with *Molinia caerulea* subsp. *arundinacea*, which has autumn leaves of orange, buff and green. It grows only 45cm (18in) tall but then throws up flowering stems topped with orange-buff seedheads which sway over the top of the earth-bound foliage. Or try a scheme using the tufted hair grass, *Deschampia cespitosa*, with tall nectaroscordum and corydalis. What you should not do is plant a load of grasses all together and call it your grass garden.

*Deschampsia cespitosa* 'Goldtau', p.88

## UNEXPECTED DELIGHTS

Autumn often brings unexpected guests. You might be able to watch a scarlet oriental poppy unfold itself from its green pod, shaking out its silk petals as you might a shirt that has been packed too long in a suitcase. This is a flower of early summer, but given the right conditions it sometimes puts on a wild late performance, too. It is only one of the perennials that finds the mild, damp weather that sometimes comes in late autumn a rather better growing proposition than early summer, the appointment we had made for it in our own rather more rigid diaries. Delphiniums often throw up late flowering spikes, too, shorter than the summer ones, but strange and welcome interlopers in an autumn melange that may be predominantly painted in shades of orange, russet and brown. Or you may get spring flowers leaping early onto the canvas, primroses perhaps or double daisies (*Bellis perennis*).

The effect is of a shambolic army, the troops all marching to different tunes. Only a few stalwarts are proceeding at the pace we expect. Some divisions that should be bringing up the rear are overtaking the leaders. Some which we thought had shot their bolt have regrouped and charged in with new ammunition. It might be a general's nightmare, but for the gardener it can be glorious – provided you do not mind throwing away the rule book. Enjoy, is the message. The show may close any day now, when winter arrives in earnest.

Mild conditions at this late season are a boon to all kinds of tender perennials such as salvias and the various types of osteospermum and argyranthmum. These opportunists will be joined by other flowers which can quite properly claim late autumn as their own season. Such is the old cottage garden chrysanthemum called 'Emperor of China', a reliably perennial chrysanthemum with soft, dirty pink flowers. The first petals are quilled, opening out to flat spoon shapes at the extremities. The centre part of the flower, still in bud, makes a dark contrast with the paler pink of the opened petals. As the flower ages, the quill effect disappears and you end up with a pale, fully double flower, spicily scented. A proper frost turns the leaves rich crimson, when it becomes even showier. Try it with brilliant blue *Salvia patens* and flowery umbels of nerine. When they have died down, it will almost be time to start looking for the first signs of winter aconites. The best gardens never have a metaphorical CLOSED sign on the gate. □

*Nerine bowdenii*, p.208

# Aconitum carmichaelii 'Arendsii' *with* Hemerocallis 'Golden Chimes' *and* Agapanthus campanulatus

Depending on the season, these three plants will probably flower in succession, the day lily (*Hemerocallis*) first, followed by the agapanthus and finally the splendid, witchy monkshood (*Aconitum*). It has a faintly sinister air about it. Take note of that, for it is extremely poisonous. That's no reason not to grow it though. There are many other things to dig up and gnaw on in the garden before you need to attack your aconitum. The flowers are of the intense deep blue we associate with delphiniums, but they are easier to grow and not so prone to slug damage. They will be happiest in cool, moist, fertile soil with some shade, but they will grow happily in full sun, provided the soil is not starved and dry. The agapanthus certainly is happier with sun on its back. Remember this when you are grouping the plants. Plants in pots, root-bound, sometimes seem to flower more freely than those in the open ground.

### Aconitum carmichaelii 'Arendsii' (Monkshood)

**Height** *1.2m (4ft).*
**Spread** *30cm (12in).*
**Flowering time** *Early autumn.*
**Star qualities** *Flowers of a most intense blue, borne in branched heads. Strong habit of growth. Excellent in cool, moist shade.*
**Other varieties** *'Kelmscott' has panicles of lavender-blue flowers; A. 'Bressingham Spire' has stems up to 90cm (36in) clothed in violet flowers; A. x cammarum 'Bicolor' has pale blue flowers washed over with whitish grey.*

### Hemerocallis 'Golden Chimes' (Day lily)

*Although each individual trumpet of a day lily lasts only one day, the plant is profligate and produces a long succession of flowers through summer. This variety has narrow leaves and star-shaped flowers of rich, deep yellow. The backs of the petals are washed over with a reddish brown. Yellows and oranges predominate in this genus and there are also some good, brick-like reds (see 'Stafford', p.146).*

### Agapanthus campanulatus

*The rough rule of thumb in choosing agapanthus is that the broader the leaf, the more tender the variety. Agapanthus campanulatus is one of the tougher species, growing up to 90cm (36in) with big, rounded umbels of flower. They can be dark or pale blue, sometimes white. There are evergreen types of agapanthus but they are difficult to overwinter in areas chillier than their South African homeland.*

*Aconitum
carmichaelii
'Arendsii'*

# Anemone x hybrida 'Honorine Jobert' *with* Dipsacus fullonum *and* Cosmos bipinnatus Sensation Mixed

Few good perennials are as easy-going as Japanese anemones. They are stayers, too. In old, abandoned gardens where brambles and couch grass have smothered all other plants, you see them still flowering profusely (often alongside old-fashioned double red peonies), repelling all boarders, defending their territory. The foliage is quite late to appear, tough vine-like leaves of a dull matt green. Then, from summer onwards, there is an astonishing succession of flowers, charmingly simple in outline, the petals gathered round a central, greenish knob. The cosmos will probably beat the anemones into flower (all depends on when they were planted out and how warm the summer has been). The tiny flowers of the teazel (*Dipsacus*), which wrap themselves in bands round the prominent head, will be completely outclassed by the other two plants. But the teazel has the last laugh, for it will be holding the stage long after the others have fled from the scene.

**Anemone x hybrida 'Honorine Jobert' (Japanese anemone)**
**Height** *1.2–1.5m (4–5ft).*
**Spread** *45cm (18in).*
**Flowering time** *Late summer to mid-autumn.*
**Star qualities** *Strong stems do not need staking. Pure white flowers are carried over a long season.*
**Other varieties** *'Géante des Blanches' has semi-double flowers, washed over with green on the reverse; 'Königin Charlotte' has large semi-double pink flowers; A. hupehensis 'Hadspen Abundance' is shorter at 90cm (36in) and has single flowers of dark pink.*

**Dipsacus fullonum (Teazel)**
*The flowers are minimal, but the thistle-like seedheads are superb and stand in good order through into winter. When fresh, the heads are pale green, but they dry to a buff-brown, still statuesque and splendid, long after the cosmos have been withered by cold. Frost only enhances the teazel, transforming the prickly bracts into sparkling bibelots. This is a biennial, but generally seeds itself around without help.*

**Cosmos bipinnatus Sensation Mixed**
*Annual cosmos, sown in spring, take time to build up to full flowering strength, so are often at their best in early autumn. The Sensation Series produces quite tall flowers, which will be a good match for the anemone. Avoid plain white varieties, which will not provide enough of a contrast. There are plenty of kinds to choose from, including a charming type called 'Sea Shells', with petals rolled round like ice-cream cones.*

*Anemone* x *hybrida*
'Honorine Jobert'

# Canna x ehemanii *with* Ricinus communis 'Impala' *and* Dahlia coccinea

Cannas are tropical beasts, most at home in the steamier parts of South America, where they grow at the margins of forests. In colder areas, they need to be treated like dahlias, the rhizomes lifted and stored through the winter. They are worth bothering with, not only on account of their vivid, late summer flowers, but also because of their leaves, huge great paddles held dramatically, like defending shields, around the flower stems. *Canna x ehemanii* is one of the best. It has enormous leaves, about 60cm (24in) long and about half as broad, smooth and shiny. They emerge as tightly rolled as a cigar, and then gradually unfold, in the dramatic way a banana leaf does. The flowers droop elegantly on their stems, unlike many other cannas, which hold their flowers in a spike rather as a gladiolus does. The colour is a rich, uncompromising pink, excellent with deeper magenta, pinkish red or purple. The canna will be out at the same time as the dahlia, so colour coordination matters. If you prefer orange-red cannas, or those with yellow-variegated leaves, choose a different dahlia.

## Canna x ehemanii
**Height** *2m (6ft).*
**Spread** *60cm (24in).*
**Flowering time** *Midsummer to early autumn.*
**Star qualities** *A richly exotic plant of statuesque form. Excellent blue-green leaves as much as 90cm (36in) long. Unusual among cannas in having hanging panicles of flowers, brilliant deep pink.*
**Other varieties** *C. glauca has narrow, glaucous foliage and lemon-coloured flowers; 'Roi Humbert' has brilliant red flowers; 'Wyoming' has brownish-purple leaves and frilled orange flowers.*

### Ricinus communis 'Impala' (Castor oil plant)
*In its North African home, this is an evergreen shrub, but gardeners in cooler climates can exploit the fact that it grows fast and use it as an exotic, leafy annual. 'Impala' has dark bronze-purple leaves, far more important than the fluffy nubs of reddish flower. The colour is subtle and the gloss on the leaf extraordinary, especially when set against other tropical exotics such as cannas.*

### Dahlia coccinea
*This Mexican species is lighter boned than most cultivars, which have wide elbows and bossy manners. It grows to about 1.2m (4ft) with single red flowers produced in an airy, branching display. They last until the first frosts. This is an enchanting, though variable, dahlia, much less dominant in mixed plantings than the beefier hybrids.*

*Canna x ehemanii* ▷

# Cimicifuga simplex 'Brunette' *with* Achillea 'Moonshine' *and* Salvia nemorosa 'Ostfriesland'

Each of these plants has great staying power. They unfold their acts slowly, but even before the flowers start to unwrap themselves, you will be able to feast on the foliage. They could scarcely be more different, the dark mounds of cimicifuga leaves contrasting with the much airier, paler foliage of the achillea. The salvia's leaves are no more than leafish, but its blue flower spikes will sing out dramatically against the cimicifuga, a thick, drenched combination of colours. With the yellow of the achillea, the blue will make a much clearer, cleaner contrast. Cimicifugas are easy in moist, well-fed soil, but resent being poked about by over-zealous gardeners. Cut down the flowered stems in late autumn and mulch the plants well in early spring. They do not require much more.

### Cimicifuga simplex 'Brunette' (Bugbane)

**Height** *1–1.2m (3–4ft).*
**Spread** *60cm (24in).*
**Flowering time** *Early to mid-autumn.*
**Star qualities** *Splendid foliage, wine dark and deeply saturated; narrow bottlebrush flowers of cream tinged with purple.*
**Other varieties** *'Elstead' is one of the latest into flower, dark green leaves and purplish buds opening to creamy white flowers; C. racemosa (Black snake root) has dark green leaves, with tall spikes of creamy-white flowers.*

### Achillea 'Moonshine'

*Mounds of feathery grey-green foliage support big flat heads of clear light yellow, not quite as palely acid as in Achillea 'Taygetea', one of the parents of 'Moonshine'. It is a neat plant, rarely reaching more than 60cm (24in) in any direction, but the flowering stems may need discreet propping with twigs of hazel. Achilleas last a long time in flower, starting in early summer and continuing until autumn.*

### Salvia nemorosa 'Ostfriesland'

*Strongly upright in habit, this salvia produces many stems, all branching out to produce flower spikes, in this case of deep violet-blue. This cultivar is not as tall as the species, and certainly not as tall as the cimicifuga, so use it towards the front of the group. The bracts surrounding the flowers are as richly coloured as the flowers themselves and they remain long after the flowers have dropped.*

*Cimicifuga simplex* 'Brunette' ▷

# Cyclamen hederifolium *with* Adiantum aleuticum *and* Crocus tommasinianus

There are very few choice, well-mannered plants that you can never have too many of. *Cyclamen hederifolium* is one of them. It has no vices and the great virtue of growing in places that other plants would spurn. You can settle it between the exposed roots of a big tree. You can use it to make a late-flowering carpet under shrubs. It puts itself away neatly at the end of its growing season, leaving only its mad seedpods, the size and colour of aniseed balls. The flowers come before the leaves, poking with surprising determination through the soil in late summer and continuing until late autumn. They have the appealing quality of small creatures heading into a gale that is too strong for them. Cyclamen do not shout at you, but it is odd how, once you have got them in the garden, you find endless excuses to go and see how they are doing. Part of their charm is that they are always doing well. Pests and diseases pass them by. The marbled leaves emerge with the last of the flowers and have the innate ability to hold themselves well and arrange themselves thoughtfully in the clump. They will still be looking good when the spring crocuses start to come up among them. The fern spins a summer thread between the two.

### Cyclamen hederifolium
**Height** *10–13cm (4–5in).*
**Spread** *15cm (6in).*
**Flowering time** *Mid- to late autumn.*
**Star qualities** *Enchanting shuttlecock flowers in various shades of pink; there is also a lovely pure white. Long-lasting leaves, roughly triangular in outline and fabulously marbled with silver.*
**Other varieties** *No other cyclamen is as easy and valuable as* C. hederifolium; *C. coum (see p.28) is good, but flowers in spring; C. purpurascens has carmine-red flowers in mid- to late summer; none of the others is truly hardy.*

### Adiantum aleuticum (Maidenhair fern)
*Use this deciduous or semi-evergreen fern with anything. It stands about 30cm (12in) high with long, thin stiff fronds, held almost horizontal. The young fronds are a pinkish sort of copper, drifting into pale green as they age. It is excellent with cyclamen and crocuses, but big enough to group with plants such as rodgersia. For most of the year, there is not a flower to be seen in groupings such as this, but the fern's slow progression through various states, always poised, holds the stage.*

### Crocus tommasinianus
*This crocus is very early, flowering from late winter into early spring. The flowers vary in colour from a pale silvery lilac to a deep, intense purple. 'Barr's Purple' (see p.106) is one of the best forms, gorgeously rich purple. Where they are suited, these crocuses increase freely both by offsets and by self-seeding. They will grow happily in grass, if it is not too coarse.*

*Cyclamen hederifolium* ▷

# Dahlia 'Grenadier' *with* Helianthus 'Gold and Silver' *and* Stipa gigantea

There are still some exquisites who sneer at dahlias, thinking them gross and vulgar. Like aspidistras and giant marrows, there is a touch of the music hall about them and even their most ardent devotees have to admit that there are some sulphurously evil yellows among them. The huge choice of flower form and colour can be perplexing, and you need to give careful thought to the varieties you choose. Dahlias planted all together in a random jumble do not dazzle. They just distract. Here a double red dahlia is used with sunflowers, the beefiness offset by the elegant waving plumes of the giant oat grass, *Stipa gigantea*. The grass will be the first plant to flower. The dahlia and sunflower will get into gear by late summer and continue until the show is brought to a crashing halt by the first frosts. Dahlias, being natives of Mexico, are tender. There's a great mystique attached to the overwintering of their tubers – the lifting, the cutting back, the dusting with flowers of sulphur, the burying in sand – but if you live in a reasonably mild area, you can forget the purist approach and leave the tubers in the ground, well mulched with leaves.

### Dahlia 'Grenadier'
**Height** *110cm (42in).*
**Spread** *60cm (24in).*
**Flowering time** *Midsummer to autumn.*
**Star qualities** *Brilliant panache; hot colour; dark foliage. Continues flowering until cut down by frost.*
**Other varieties** *'Hillcrest Royal' has spiky petals of magenta swirling out from a tightly buttoned centre; 'Hamari Gold' has flowers like whirling suns; 'David Howard' has neat, rich orange flowers set against dark bronze foliage.*

### Helianthus 'Gold and Silver' (Sunflower)
*This is an annual sunflower, growing incredibly quickly from seed to produce stems that will top the dahlia, but not by too much. This is not the place for real giants such as 'Taiyo', which grows up to 3m (10ft) tall. On 'Gold and Silver' the flowers are gold, the foliage silvery. For a richer, more saturated combination, choose a mahogany-coloured sunflower such as 'Prado Red', which carries a multitude of flowers on stems no more than 1.5m (5ft) high.*

### Stipa gigantea (Giant oat grass)
*A native of Spain and Portugal, the foliage of this oat grass makes a dense, weed-suppressing clump about 70cm (28in) high. From this underpinning come elegant waving stems of oatish flowers which shoot up to 2.5m (8ft) where suited. When they first unfold, they are a purplish green, but they gradually bleach as they ripen to a soft straw colour. Though tall, they are strong and never need staking.*

*Dahlia* 'Grenadier'

# Geranium wallichianum 'Buxton's Variety'
*with* Cleome hassleriana 'Violet Queen' *and* Colchicum agrippinum

Blues and purplish pinks predominate in this particular selection, but by choosing different varieties of any of the three flowers, you can make it pinker. Or paler. If you use the geranium 'Buxton's Variety' you will have three flowers out at the same time, but if it suits you better to have action earlier in the season, choose a geranium such as 'Mrs Kendall Clark' (*see below, right*) that comes into flower in early summer. Colchicums have quite coarse leaves which make big, congested clumps, but one of the advantages of *C. agrippinum* is that its leaves are much less beefy than those of the more commonly planted 'Autumn Queen'. The geranium 'Buxton's Variety' has a wandering habit, its long trailing stems creeping stealthily through surrounding plants. Make sure none of the stems lie on top of the colchicums as they emerge. The cleome will tower over the other two plants, but the geranium can clamber up into the lower reaches of its stems, where it looks very appealing.

### Geranium wallichianum 'Buxton's Variety'
**Height** *30cm (12in).*
**Spread** *1.2m (4ft).*
**Flowering time** *Late summer to autumn.*
**Star qualities** *Attractive lobed and toothed leaves. Sky blue flowers with white centres produced over a long season. Spreads generously but does not root as it goes.*
**Other varieties** *'Ann Folkard' has magenta flowers with black centres; G. himalayense 'Gravetye' has blue flowers over foliage that colours well in autumn; 'Johnson's Blue' produces saucer-shaped blue flowers, but only during summer; G. x magnificum has flowers of rich saturated purplish blue, but only at midsummer; G. pratense 'Mrs Kendall Clark' has stripy blue-grey flowers on tall, rangy plants, but only in early summer.*

### Cleome hassleriana 'Violet Queen' (Spider flower)
*Cleome is an annual that looks as though it should be a perennial for it produces vast amounts of growth in a season. The leaves are exceptionally handsome, cut into deep-fingered lobes. When well-grown, the flowering stems reach 1.5m (5ft), and the spider legs that stick out all round the flowerhead will later bear seedpods. Cleomes fill the pink and purple part of the spectrum, running from white to a deep magenta. 'Violet Queen' is a deep pinkish purple.*

### Colchicum agrippinum (Autumn crocus)
*The flowers leap through the ground in autumn, making elegant long-stemmed goblets. The leaves follow much later, forming surprisingly large clumps, which last until midsummer of the following season. This species has flowers 8–10cm (3–4in) high of a deep, purplish pink, checked or "tessellated" with a paler colour in the way that snake's head fritillaries are.*

# Nerine bowdenii *with* Papaver rhoeas 'Mother of Pearl' *and* Aster x frikartii 'Mönch'

The nerine will be the last plant to come into flower in this group, which will start with the poppies in midsummer, and then continue with the aster. That will still be in flower by the time the nerine appears. So a long succession of colour will be produced by this threesome, but not all at the same time. Nerines are not fully hardy (this species comes from South Africa) and do best where they can be planted at the base of a sunny wall. Plant shallowly, so that the noses of the bulbs are just above ground. Like colchicums, they flower without their leaves. The strappy foliage follows later and does not die down until the following summer. The poppies are gorgeous, but being used to having corn to prop them up on all sides, will probably need some discreet staking to keep them upright. Sow seed in early autumn, rather than in spring. The easiest way is to sow where the poppies are to flower.

### Nerine bowdenii
**Height** *45cm (18in).*
**Spread** *8cm (3in).*
**Flowering time** *Autumn.*
**Star qualities** *Rounded heads of pink trumpet flowers like small lilies. Late starting into flower, when so many other garden plants are finishing.*
**Other varieties** *N.* sarniensis *'Alba' has pure white flowers and deep green leaves, and can be grown outside in favoured, well-drained spots.*

### Papaver rhoeas 'Mother of Pearl' (Field poppy)
*This selection of the annual field poppy was raised by the painter Sir Cedric Morris in his garden at Benton End, Suffolk. From the plain red field poppy, he conjured up a marvellous strain of flowers in grey, dirty pink and lavender, many of them double. They have the strange texture of tissue paper left out in the rain. Conserve the best colours by marking them, and allowing only these plants to set seed. In the right conditions this poppy is a vigorous self-seeder.*

### Aster x frikartii 'Mönch'
*One of the best of all asters, lasting a very long time in flower from midsummer to autumn. It was raised by M. Frikart in Switzerland around 1920 and named after a neighbouring mountain. The daisy flowers are about as blue as an aster gets and each has a central fluffy knob of yellow. Though it grows to 70cm (28in), it does not need staking.*

*Nerine bowdenii*

# Polypodium interjectum 'Cornubiense' *with* Hosta 'Vera Verde' *and* Meconopsis cambrica

The common polypody is a plain fern, made up of a stiffish midrib with simple leaflets sprouting along it at regular intervals, but there are many different variations on the theme, including *Polypodium cambricum*. This was first discovered near Cardiff, in south Wales, in 1668. 'Cornubiense' does not have such rarefied pedigree, but spreads to make excellent ground cover. The fronds are wider, lacier than the common polypody, a bright fresh green and so deeply divided as to look like lace. Most ferns unfurl their fresh fronds in late spring. This one saves its freshest clothes for late summer, when other plants are beginning to look tired and dusty. It colonizes well, the fleshy rhizomes creeping slowly across ground in sun or partial shade. It will put up with quite dry growing conditions but is lusher (as you would expect) in damp, rich soil. The polypody will get along in any company but is particularly good with the hosta. Its mounds of finely cut leaves contrast tellingly with the solid, fleshy foliage of *Hosta* 'Vera Verde'. The meconopsis adds a smattering of flowers from early summer to early autumn.

*Polypodium interjectum 'Cornubiense'* (Common polypody)
**Height** *30–40cm (12–16in).*
**Spread** *30–40cm (12–16in).*
**Star qualities** *Evergreen; excellent ground cover, especially in slightly difficult dry areas; new foliage appears in late summer, when fresh green leaves are most welcome.*
**Other varieties** P. cambricum *has the same habit of producing new fronds in late summer, but they die back again in spring;* P. cambricum *'Cristatum' has fronds with crests on the tips and at the ends of the pinnae.*

### Hosta 'Vera Verde'

*Small enough to be in scale with its companions in this group, the fern and the Welsh poppy, the leaves of this hosta are a matt mid-green, thinly outlined with cream. It has pale mauve flowers, striped with a deeper purple. Like most hostas, it is better with some shade. That won't upset the poppy or the fern at all.*

### Meconopsis cambrica (Welsh poppy)

*A less showy garden flower than the fabulous blue-flowered meconopsis of the Himalayas, but a charming self-seeding perennial, in form very like the annual field poppy. But no field poppy produces flowers of orange and yellow, which this little meconopsis does. And it is as happy in the shade as in sun, a useful trait. It rarely grows more than 45cm (18in) tall, with deeply dissected bluish-green leaves.*

*Polypodium interjectum*
'Cornubiense'

# Verbena bonariensis *with* Tagetes 'Vanilla' *and* Kale 'Redbor'

Most perennials fuss about too long with their leaves before they even think of tossing you a flower. *Verbena bonariensis* gets straight on with the job. Most of its leaves are clustered in a smallish basal rosette. From this rises a tall, immensely thin but branching stem. You never get tired of it for it is delicate (but not so much as to be overpowered by the kale which is its companion here) and the colour is obliging enough to fit in with whatever is going on around it. It does not even need deadheading, as the flowers all push out in succession from the same starting point. Plants are devoted self-seeders, so, once introduced, they never want to leave. Even if they seed into the foreground of a planting, they are welcome, because the plants are so thin that the effect is like looking through a bead curtain at whatever lies beyond. The kale gives bulk to the group and, being relatively hardy, will stand on through winter, when the sun-loving marigolds (*Tagetes*) have melted away. Other vegetables, such as coloured chard, look equally good with summer annuals.

**Verbena bonariensis**
**Height** *To 2m (6ft).*
**Spread** *45cm (18in).*
**Flowering time** *Midsummer to early autumn.*
**Star qualities** *Thin, graceful habit, all stem and no leaf. Charming topknots of tiny purple flowers, jammed together in a head. They come out individually, to give an exceptionally long flowering period.*
**Other varieties** *No other verbena has the same useful, upright habit but there are many pretty, half-hardy cultivars such as 'Lawrence Johnston', with bright red flowers, and 'Sissinghurst', a prostrate type with magenta-pink flowers.*

### *Tagetes* 'Vanilla' (African marigold)

*There are many different kinds of African and French marigold that would work with the deep saturated purple of the verbena and the kale, but the best will be those that are tall, with big flowers on the acid yellow side of the spectrum. The orange and striped kinds would provide too harsh a contrast. 'Vanilla' grows to 35cm (14in) and produces its pale sherbet-coloured flowers from early summer to late autumn.*

### Kale 'Redbor'

*Kale (Brassica oleracea) is not the only vegetable that is handsome enough to be used in the flower garden. Dark, frilly lettuces look good in mixed plantings, too. But this F1 hybrid kale will not be dwarfed by the verbena, and is highly decorative with its crinkled purple-red leaves. You will need to sow seed, grow the young plants on in a row and transplant them into their final positions with a good ball of soil round their roots.*

*Verbena bonariensis*

IN THE PRECEDING CHAPTERS, the star plants for each season have all been given two ideal partners, to create planting combinations that either provide a satisfying succession of interest through the year, or, where flowering times coincide, an eye-catching burst of colour. These "off-the-peg" planting recipes have

# alternative partners

been designed to suit all sorts of sites and soils as well as all kinds of gardens. But you may also find they inspire you to create slightly different schemes, tailored to suit your own particular needs or tastes, and the following lists suggest additional good companions for each of the star plants, arranged here in alphabetical rather than seasonal order.

### Pattern of leaves
*Foliage contrasts give long-lasting pleasure in a garden, as here where variegated Silybum marianum combines with the thread-like leaves of fennel.*

*Aconitum carmichaelii*
'Arendsii'
*(p.194) with...*

Aster novae-angliae 'Pink Lace'
*Cimicifuga simplex*
*Dipsacus fullonum*
*Helenium autumnale*
Helianthus 'Capenoch Star'
*Kniphofia triangularis*
*Leucanthamella serotina*
Macleaya 'Spetchley Ruby'
*Persicaria orientalis*
Phlox paniculata 'White Admiral'
Rudbeckia hirta 'Indian Summer'
*Sinacalia tangutica (syn. Senecio*
  *tanguticus)*

*Allium giganteum*
*(p.138) with...*

*Agapanthus caulescens*
Anemone x hybrida 'Honorine
  Jobert'
*Artemisia stelleriana*
*Aster sedifolius*
Cerinthe major 'Purpurascens'
Chaerophyllum hirsutum 'Roseum'
Eremurus x isabellinus 'Cleopatra'
*Gladiolus communis* subsp.
  *byzantinus*
Lupins (blue)
Nepeta 'Six Hills Giant'
*Nigella damascena*
*Paeonia mascula* subsp. *arietina*
*Papaver somniferum*
Polemonium caeruleum 'Brise
  d'Anjou'
Irises (bearded)
Salvia viridis 'Blue Beard'
*Sedum spectabile*
Silene dioica 'Flore Pleno'
*Smyrnium perfoliatum*
*Zigadenus elegans*

*Anemone* x *hybrida*
'Honorine Jobert'
*(p.196) with...*

Ageratum 'Blue Horizon'
*Allium cristophii*
*Athyrium filix-femina*
Crocus chrysanthus 'Zwanenburg
  Bronze'
Iris 'Purple Sensation' (Dutch)
Lamium maculatum 'White Nancy'
*Lilium pyrenaicum*
Salvia involucrata 'Bethellii'
Tulipa 'Abba'
*Verbena bonariensis*

*Aquilegia vulgaris*
'Nora Barlow'
*(p. 70)* *with…*

Allium giganteum
Anemone coronaria 'Lord
   Lieutenant'
Antirrhinum 'White Wonder'
Campanula persicifolia 'Pride of
   Exmouth'
Colchicum 'Lilac Wonder'
Crocus corsicus
Dianthus deltoides
Dicentra formosa
Ferula communis
Foxgloves, white (Digitalis)
Geranium 'Ann Folkard'
Gypsophila repens 'Dorothy
   Teacher'
Hyacinthus orientalis 'Carnegie'
Irises (bearded)
Iris sibirica
Lupins
Myosotis sylvatica 'Ultramarine'
Narcissus 'Ice Wings'
Nepeta 'Souvenir d'André
   Chaudron'
Tulipa 'Couleur Cardinal'

*Arum italicum* 'Marmoratum'
*(p.24)* *with…*

Astilbe x arendsii 'Brautschleier'
Fritillaria meleagris
Galanthus elwesii
Gentiana asclepiadea
Geranium cinereum 'Ballerina'
Helleborus orientalis
Iris foetidissima var. citrina
Meconopsis cambrica
Milium effusum 'Aureum'
Narcissus 'Cedric Morris'
Polypodium cambricum
   'Cambricum'
Primula vulgaris
Ranunculus 'Brazen Hussy'
Scilla bithynica

*Asplenium scolopendrium*
*(p.26)* *with…*

Anemone blanda 'White
   Splendour'
Asarum europaeum
Athyrium filix-femina
Carex oshimensis 'Evergold'
Crocus banaticus
Cyclamen hederifolium
Hosta crispula
Narcissus 'Jenny'
Polygonatum x hybridum
Scilla siberica

*Astrantia major* 'Shaggy'
*(p.140) with…*

Asplenium scolopendrium
Cardamine pratensis 'Flore Pleno'
Cimicifuga simplex Atropurpurea
   Group
Iris 'Golden Harvest' (Dutch)
Lagurus ovatus
Narcissus 'Saint Keverne'
Nicotiana x sanderae 'Fragrant
   Cloud'
Primula vulgaris Barnhaven Blues
   Group
Pulmonaria 'Lewis Palmer'
Scilla bifolia
Viola riviniana Purpurea Group

*Campanula latiloba*
'Hidcote Amethyst'
*(p.142) with…*

Achillea 'Moonshine'
Aruncus dioicus
Euphorbia palustris
Galega orientalis
Lavatera trimestris 'Mont Blanc'
Lilium candidum
Lilium x testaceum
Peonia lactiflora 'Festiva Maxima'
Pimpinella major 'Rosea'
Tulipa 'Estella Rijnveld'

*Canna* x *ehemanii*
*(p.198) with…*

Amaranthus 'Intense Purple'
Arundo donax var. versicolor
Cortaderia selloana 'Pumila'
Cosmos bipinnatus 'Dazzler'
Cynara cardunculus
Dahlia 'Alltami Corsair'
Dahlia 'Wittemans Superba'
Leymus arenarius
Lobelia 'Dark Crusader'
Phormium 'Sundowner'
Plectranthus argentatus
Ricinus communis 'Carmencita'
Salvia involucrata 'Bethellii'
Salvia uliginosa
Schizostylis coccinea
Stipa tenuissima
Tulipa 'Alabaster'
Verbena bonariensis
Zinnia Allsorts

*Cerinthe major* 'Purpurascens'
(p.144) *with...*

*Allium carinatum* subsp.
  *pulchellum*
*Anemone coronaria* 'The Admiral'
*Camassia leichtlinii*
*Crocus chrysanthus* 'Blue Pearl'
*Fritillaria persica* 'Adiyaman'
*Gladiolus communis* subsp.
  *byzantinus*
*Hordeum jubatum*
*Iris* 'H.C. van Vliet' (Dutch)
*Narcissus* x *odorus* 'Double
  Campernelle'
*Osteospermum* 'Buttermilk'
*Smyrnium perfoliatum*

*Cimifuga simplex* 'Brunette'
(p.200) *with...*

*Aconitum carmichaelii*
*Argyranthemum* 'Jamaica
  Primrose'
*Aster ericoides*
*Astilbe* x *arendsii* 'Brautschleier'
*Darmera peltata* (syn. *Peltiphyllum
  peltatum*)
*Dipsacus fullonum*
*Francoa sonchifolia*
*Iris pseudacorus* 'Variegata'
*Kniphofia galpinii*
*Persicaria amplexicaulis* 'Alba'

*Convallaria majalis*
(p.72) *with...*

*Galanthus* 'John Gray'
*Hepatica nobilis*
*Hyacinthoides non-scripta*
  (bluebell)
*Iris* 'Grapesicle'
*Lunaria annua*
*Matteuccia struthiopteris*
*Muscari armeniacum* 'Blue Spike'
*Myosotis* (forget-me-not)
*Primula denticulata*
*Pulmonaria saccharata*

*Crambe cordifolia*
(p.74) *with...*

Canna 'Durban'
Dahlia 'Rip City'
Delphinium 'Emily Hawkins'
Epilobium hirsutum 'Well Creek'
Foeniculum vulgare 'Purpureum'
Osmunda regalis 'Purpurascens'
Papaver orientale Goliath Group
Pennisetum alopecuroides
  'Hameln'
Romneya coulteri
Tulipa 'Halcro'
Verbascum olympicum

*Crocosmia* 'Lucifer'
(p.146) *with...*

Allium cristophii
Artemisia stelleriana 'Boughton
  Silver'
Aster sedifolius
Atriplex hortensis var. rubra
Bupleurum falcatum
Coreopsis verticillata
Dahlia 'Tally Ho'
Eryngium x oliverianum
Foeniculum vulgare
Hemerocallis 'Green Flutter'
Kniphofia rooperi
Kniphofia uvaria 'Nobilis'
Papaver commutatum
Physalis alkekengi var. franchetii
Ranunculus ficaria 'Brazen Hussy'
Sanguisorba tenuifolia 'Alba'

*Cyclamen coum*
(p.28) *with...*

Anemone blanda 'Ingramii'
Crocus tommasinianus
Epimedium grandiflorum
Fritillaria pyrenaica
Helleborus argutifolius
Iris 'Apollo' (Dutch)
Muscari armeniacum 'Blue Spike'
Narcissus 'Hawera'
Saxifraga x urbium
Tulipa humilis

*Cyclamen hederifolium*
(p.202) *with…*

Anemone blanda 'Ingramii'
Anomatheca laxa
Asplenium scolopendrium Crispum
   Group
Blechnum penna-marina
Brimeura amethystina
Chionodoxa forbesii 'Pink Giant'
Corydalis solida
Eranthis hyemalis
Erythronium californicum
Fritillaria michailovskyi
Galanthus reginae-olgae
   'Cambridge'
Geranium wallichianum 'Buxton's
   Variety'
Iris reticulata 'Harmony'
Leucojum vernum
Muscari comosum 'Plumosum'
Narcissus 'Jumblie'
Ornithogalum nutans
Oxalis triangularis
Scilla bifolia
Triteleia laxa

*Dahlia* 'Grenadier'
(p.204) *with…*

Amaranthus caudatus
Arundo donax var. versicolor
Aster lateriflorus 'Horizontalis'
Canna 'Roi Humbert'
Dipsacus fullonum
Iris 'Royal Yellow' (Dutch)
Kniphofia 'Bees' Sunset'
Ricinus communis
Rudbeckia amplexicaulis
Salvia guaranitica 'Blue Enigma'
Verbena bonariensis

*Delphinium grandiflorum*
'Blue Butterfly'
(p.148) *with…*

Crocus chrysanthus 'Cream
   Beauty'
Hemerocallis lilioasphodelus
Iris reticulata 'Harmony'
Lilium Pink Perfection Group
Nigella hispanica
Paeonia lactiflora 'Lady
   Alexandra Duff'
Papaver orientale 'Aglaja'
Scrophularia auriculata 'Variegata'
Thalictrum speciosissimum
Tulipa 'Groenland'

*Dianthus* 'Dad's Favourite'
*(p.150) with...*

Agapanthus campanulatus subsp.
  patens
Anagallis monellii subsp. linifolia
Aquilegia 'Hensol Harebell'
Armeria juniperifolia 'Bevan's
  Variety'
Aubrieta x cultorum 'Joy'
Crocus chrysanthus 'E.A. Bowles'
Gladiolus callianthus 'Murieliae'
Lagurus ovatus
Phlox douglasii 'Boothman's
  Variety'
Triteleia laxa 'Koningin Fabiola'
Tulipa eichleri
  (syn. T. undulatifolia)

*Dicentra* 'Stuart Boothman'
*(p.76) with...*

Actaea spicata
Aegopodium podagraria
  'Variegatum'
Anemone x hybrida 'Profusion'
Colchicum 'Waterlily'
Cyclamen hederifolium
Epimedium grandiflorum 'Nanum'
Euphorbia polychroma
Gentiana asclepiadea
Gladiolus tristris
Glaucidium palmatum
Hosta undulata var. albomarginata
  (syn. H. 'Thomas Hogg')
Kirengeshoma palmata
Lilium formosanum
Meconopsis x sheldonii 'Slieve
  Donard'
Milium effusum 'Aureum'
Nomocharis aperta
Polygonatum x hybridum
Primula 'Bronwyn'
Primula capitata subsp. mooreana

*Digitalis purpurea*
Excelsior Group
*(p.152) with...*

Anemone x hybrida 'September
  Charm'
Cimicifuga simplex 'Brunette'
Geranium 'Ann Folkard'
Hosta undulata var. univittata
Ligularia przewalskii
Lilium 'Rosemary North'
Matteuccia struthiopteris
Miscanthus sinensis 'Silberfeder'
Primula beesiana
Rodgersia podophylla

*Dryopteris wallichiana*
(p.78) *with…*

Asarum europaeum
Asplenium scolopendrium
Athyrium niponicum var. pictum
Begonia grandis subsp. evansiana
Cyrtomium falcatum
Galanthus 'Magnet'
Hosta sieboldiana
Matteuccia struthiopteris
Meconopsis cambrica
Polystichum setiferum
Pulmonaria saccharata Argentea
  Group
Saxifraga fortunei
Scilla mischtschenkoana
  'Tubergeniana'
Sinacalia tangutica
Trillium grandiflorum 'Flore Pleno'

*Eryngium giganteum*
(p.154) *with…*

Anthemis tinctoria 'E.C. Buxton'
Asphodeline liburnica
Coreopsis verticillata 'Grandiflora'
Crambe maritima
Crocosmia x crocosmiiflora
  'Solfaterre'
Geranium pratense 'Plenum
  Violaceum'
Gillenia trifoliata
Hemerocallis 'Stella d'Oro'
Lychnis coronaria
Kale 'Redbor'
Narcissus cyclamineus
Osteospermum 'Pink Whirls'
Phlomis russeliana
Romneya coulteri

*Erythronium* 'Pagoda'
(p.30) *with…*

Ajuga reptans 'Catlin's Giant'
Arum italicum 'Marmoratum'
Crocus cartwrightianus
Kirengeshoma palmata
Lamium maculatum 'Beacon
  Silver'
Matteuccia struthiopteris
Omphalodes cappadocica
Primula chionantha
Pulmonaria angustifolia
Scilla bifolia

*Eschscholzia californica*
(p. 156) *with...*

Armeria maritima 'Alba'
Campanula glomerata 'Superba'
Crocus chrysanthus 'Snow
   Bunting'
Dianthus 'Haytor White'
Hyacinthus 'Hollyhock'
Iris 'Hildegarde' (Dutch)
Lagurus ovatus
Lettuce 'Lollo Rosso'
Pennisetum villosum
Tulipa humilis 'Persian Pearl'

*Euphorbia characias*
(p. 80) *with...*

Asarum europaeum
Bergenia cordifolia 'Purpurea'
Galanthus 'S. Arnott'
Helleborus niger
Helleborus orientalis
Hosta 'Jade Cascade'
Iris histrioides 'Major'
Kniphofia 'Alcazar'
Miscanthus sinensis 'Adagio'
Narcissus 'Barnum'
Romneya coulteri
Rudbeckia 'Herbstsonne'
Salvia uliginosa
Tulipa 'Queen of Sheba'

*Euphorbia myrsinites*
(p. 32) *with...*

Antirrhinum majus 'Black Prince'
Bergenia stracheyi
Campanula portenschlagiana
Crocus angustifolius
Eryngium bourgatii
Lamium maculatum
Milium effusum 'Aureum'
Persicaria virginiana 'Painter's
   Palette' (syn. Tovara)
Scilla bifolia
Tulipa 'Bellona'

## Geranium psilostemon
(p.158) with…

Agapanthus (white)
Allium giganteum
Alstroemeria ligtu hybrids
Anthemis punctata subsp.
  cupaniana
Anthericum liliago
Aquilegia vulgaris 'William
  Guiness'
Artemisia absinthium 'Lambrook
  Mist'
Arundo donax
Camassia leichtlinii subsp.
  leichtlinii
Crambe cordifolia
Crocus speciosus
Dicentra 'Langtrees'
Eryngium alpinum
Hedychium densiflorum
Irises (tall purple bearded)
Lilium pyrenaicum
Matthiola incana (Brompton
  stock)
Polemonium 'Lambrook Mauve'

## Geranium wallichianum
'Buxton's Variety'
(p.206) with…

Allium caeruleum
Alstroemeria ligtu hybrids
Anthemis sancti-johannis
Anthericum liliago
Aquilegia 'Hensol Harebell'
Artemisia absinthium 'Lambrook
  Mist'
Camassia leichtlinii subsp.
  leichtlinii
Clematis integrifolia
Crambe cordifolia
Dicentra 'Langtrees'
Eryngium alpinum
Gladiolus 'The Bride'
Hedychium densiflorum
Hemerocallis 'Golden Chimes'
Iris reticulata
Lilium pyrenaicum
Ranunculus acris 'Stevenii'
Sedum 'Ruby Glow'
Sisyrinchium striatum
Thermopsis rhombifolia var.
  montana

## Gladiolus communis
subsp. byzantinus
(p.82) with…

Allium schubertii
Aquilegia vulgaris 'Magpie'
Baptisia australis
Cerinthe major 'Purpurascens'
Clematis recta 'Purpurea'
Foeniculum vulgare 'Purpureum'
Geranium 'Bertie Crûg'
Iris x robusta 'Gerald Darby'
Lunaria annua
Matthiola incana (Brompton
  stock)
Myosotis sylvestris
Nectaroscordum siculum
Nerine bowdenii
Paeonia lactiflora 'Marie Lemoine'
Phlox paniculata 'Eventide'
Silybum marianum
Smyrnium perfoliatum
Tulipa 'Bleu Aimable'

*Helenium*
'Moerheim Beauty'
*(p.160) with...*

*Aconitum carmichaelii* 'Kelmscott'
*Amaranthus caudatus*
*Canna* 'Durban'
*Cimicifuga racemosa* 'Purpurea'
*Kniphofia rooperi*
*Lobelia* 'Dark Crusader'
*Macleaya cordata*
*Physalis alkekengi* var. *franchetii*
*Salvia* x *superba*
*Stipa tenuissima*
*Tulipa* 'Madame Lefeber'

*Helleborus orientalis*
*(p.34) with...*

*Aconitum* x *cammarum* 'Bicolor'
*Arum italicum* 'Marmoratum'
*Crocus tommasinianus* 'Ruby
  Giant'
*Epimedium grandiflorum* 'Nanum'
*Eranthis hyemalis* 'Guinea Gold'
*Euphorbia characias* subsp.
  *wulfenii*
*Galanthus* 'Atkinsii'
*Milium effusum* 'Aureum'
*Narcissus* 'February Gold'
*Primula frondosa*

*Hemerocallis* 'Citrina'
*(p.162) with...*

*Alstroemeria aurea*
*Echinops ritro*
*Eryngium* x *oliverianum*
*Geranium* 'Johnson's Blue'
*Lupins*
*Narcissus* 'Geranium'
*Phlox paniculata*
*Ricinus communis* 'Carmencita'
*Rudbeckia* 'Goldquelle'
*Salvia farinacea* 'Victoria'

*Hosta* 'Krossa Regal'
(p.164) *with…*

Anemone hupehensis 'Prinz
   Heinrich'
Astelia chathamica
Astilboides tabularis
Athyrium filix-femina
Delphinium 'Gillian Dallas'
Echinacea purpurea
Filpendula rubra 'Venusta'
Helianthus decapetalus 'Triomphe
   de Gand'
Helleborus argutifolius
Heuchera americana Dale's Strain
Kirengeshoma palmata
Lilium 'Rosemary North'
Persicaria amplexicaule
   'Atrosanguinea'
Phlox paniculata 'Le Mahdi'
Rodgersia pinnata 'Elegans'
Smilacina racemosa
Stachys byzantina 'Primrose
   Heron'
Stipa tenuissima
Veratrum album
Verbascum chaixii 'Cotswold
   Beauty'

*Hyacinthus orientalis*
'King Codro'
(p.36) *with…*

Antirrhinum 'Night and Day'
Aquilegia coerulea
Euphorbia amygdaloides var.
   robbiae
Geranium cinereum var.
   subcaulescens 'Splendens'
Hemerocallis 'Stoke Poges'
Hosta 'Francee'
Iris 'Casa Blanca' (Dutch)
Lathyrus vernus
Narcissus 'Baby Moon'
Tulipa 'Berlioz'

*Iris* 'Jane Phillips'
(p.84) *with…*

Allium hollandicum 'Purple
   Sensation'
Aster cordifolius 'Chieftain'
Crocus tommasinianus
Dactylorhiza elata
Dicentra spectabilis 'Alba'
Eremurus aitchisonii 'Albus'
Euphorbia nicaeensis
Hemerocallis lilioasphodelus
Lamium orvala
Lysimachia ciliata 'Firecracker'
Tulipa 'China Pink'

*Iris sibirica*
(p.86) *with...*

Aster novae-angliae 'Barr's Violet'
Astrantia major 'Hadspen Blood'
Eupatorium rugosum 'Chocolate'
Euphorbia griffithii
Francoa sonchifolia 'Dr Tom
  Smith'
Galega 'His Majesty'
Geranium pratense Victor Reiter
  Strain
Hemerocallis 'Corky'
Heuchera 'Raspberry Regal'
Hosta 'Frances Williams'
Inula acaulis
Knautia macedonica
Kniphofia 'Drummore Apricot'
Lathyrus vernus 'Spring Melody'
Leucanthemum x superbum 'Fiona
  Coghill'
Lilium lancifolium
Mertensia pulmonarioides
Osteospermum 'Joe Elliott'
Papaver orientale 'Cedric Morris'
Penstemon 'Alice Hindley'
Tulipa 'Bleu Aimable'

*Leucojum aestivum*
'Gravetye Giant'
(p.38) *with...*

Anemone blanda 'White
  Splendour'
Corydalis flexuosa 'Père David'
Epimedium x versicolor
  'Neosulphureum'
Euphorbia dulcis 'Chameleon'
Helleborus orientalis
Matteuccia struthiopteris
Scilla bifolia
Tulipa linifolia Batalinii Group
  'Bronze Charm'
Valeriana phu 'Aurea'
Viola 'Beshlie'

*Lilium regale*
(p.166) *with...*

Antirrhinum majus 'Black Prince'
Campanula lactiflora 'Superba'
Cosmos bipinnatus
Delphinium 'Emily Hawkins'
Eucomis pole-evansii
Paeonia cambessedesii
Phlox paniculata 'Eventide'
Polemonium foliosissimum
Primula florindae
Tulipa 'Alfred Cortot'
Veratrum nigrum

*Narcissus* 'Quail'
*(p.40) with...*

Athyrium niponicum var. pictum
Danae racemosa
Doronicum orientale
Eryngium alpinum 'Amethyst'
Erythronium californicum 'White
  Beauty'
Helleborus argutifolius
Hemerocallis 'Beloved Returns'
Hyacinthus orientalis 'Ostara'
Iris histriodes 'Major'
Romneya coulteri
Tulipa montana
  (syn. T. chrysantha)
Veronica peduncularis 'Georgia
  Blue'
Viola 'Aspasia'

*Nectaroscordum siculum*
*(p.88) with...*

Aconitum carmichaelii 'Arendsii'
Agapanthus Ardernei hybrid
Alstroemeria aurea
Astilbe 'Inshriach Pink'
Euphorbia seguieriana
Ferula communis subsp. glauca
Galtonia princeps
Gaura lindheimeri
Geranium macrorrhizum 'Album'
Gladiolus communis subsp.
  byzantinus
Hedychium greenei
Helenium 'Sahin's Early Flowerer'
Hemerocallis 'Chicago Royal Robe'
Heuchera micrantha 'Martha
  Roderick'
Hosta 'Sum and Substance'
Iris orientalis
Kniphofia 'Barton Fever'
Leucojum aestivum 'Gravetye
  Giant'
Paeonia mascula subsp. arietina
Pennisetum orientale

*Nepeta* 'Six Hills Giant'
*(p.168) with...*

Allium giganteum
Clematis integrifolia
Eryngium alpinum
Geranium 'Johnson's Blue'
Gillenia trifoliata
Hosta 'Wide Brim'
Iris 'Sapphire Beauty' (Dutch)
Nicotiana langsdorfii
Papaver somniferum 'Black
  Beauty'
Tulipa 'Abu Hassan'
Verbascum chaixii 'Gainsborough'

*Nerine bowdenii*
*(p.208) with…*

Agapanthus inapertus subsp.
 pendulus
Anaphalis triplinervis
Aster amellus 'Veilchenönigin'
Cosmos bipinnatus
Crocus medius
Iris 'Symphony' (Dutch)
Liriope muscari
Lychnis coronaria
Sedum telephium subsp. maximum
 'Atropurpureum'
Verbena bonariensis
Zephyranthes candida

*Nigella damascena* 'Miss Jekyll'
*(p.170) with…*

Alchemilla mollis
Allium cristophii
Eryngium bourgatii 'Oxford Blue'
Erysimum cheiri 'Ruby Gem'
Geranium wallichianum 'Buxton's
 Variety'
Irises (bearded)
Lagurus ovatus
Meconopsis cambrica
Nicotiana 'Lime Green'
Papaver somniferum 'Pink Chiffon'
Zinnia 'Envy'

*Osmunda regalis*
*(p.90) with…*

Arum italicum 'Marmoratum'
Astilboides tabularis
Brunnera macrophylla 'Hadspen
 Cream'
Caltha palustris 'Flore Pleno'
Carex oshimensis 'Evergold'
Corydalis solida f. transsylvanica
 'George Baker'
Fritillaria meleagris
Galanthus nivalis
Hosta 'Blue Angel'
Iris pseudacorus
Rheum palmatum 'Hadspen
 Crimson'
Sanguisorba menziesii
Saxifraga 'Miss Chambers'
Scrophularia auriculata 'Variegata'
Smilacina racemosa
Symphytum x uplandicum
 'Variegatum'
Trillium grandiflorum
Uvularia grandiflora

*Paeonia lactiflora*
'Bowl of Beauty'
*(p.92) with...*

Anemone x *hybrida* 'Whirlwind'
*Antirrhinum majus* 'Black Prince'
*Aquilegia vulgaris* var. *stellata*
  'Greenapples'
*Aster* 'Little Carlow'
*Camassia quamash* 'Blue Melody'
*Campanula* 'Kent Belle'
*Centaurea cineraria*
*Cerinthe major* 'Purpurascens'
*Corydalis flexuosa* 'Nightshade'
*Delphinium* 'Blue Dawn'
*Fritillaria imperialis*
*Galtonia candicans*
*Gladiolius* 'The Bride'
*Hyacinthus orientalis* 'Anna Marie'
*Ipheion uniflorum*
*Narcissus* 'Empress of Ireland'
*Narcissus* 'Merlin'
*Saxifraga* x *urbium*
*Tulipa* 'Blue Parrot'
*Zinnia* Allsorts

*Papaver orientale* 'Patty's Plum'
*(p.94) with...*

*Allium hollandicum* 'Purple
  Sensation'
*Anthriscus sylvestris* 'Ravenswing'
*Crinum* x *powellii* 'Album'
*Crocosmia* 'Gerbe d'Or'
*Crocus etruscus* 'Zwanenburg'
*Cynara cardunculus*
*Dahlia* 'Bednall Beauty'
*Delphinium* 'Summerfield Oberon'
*Dierama dracomontanum*
*Gypsophila paniculata*
*Macleaya* 'Spetchley Ruby'
*Thalictrum flavum* 'Illuminator'
*Tulipa* 'Annie Schilder'

*Phlox carolina* 'Miss Lingard'
*(p.172) with...*

*Astilbe chinensis* var. *taquetii*
  'Superba'
*Calamagrostis* x *acutiflora*
  'Overdam'
*Helianthus salicifolius*
*Hemerocallis* 'Marion Vaughn'
*Iris* 'Ideal' (Dutch)
*Papaver rhoeas* 'Mother of Pearl'
*Persicaria orientalis*
*Stachys byzantina* 'Primrose
  Heron'
*Tulipa marjolletii*
*Verbascum olympicum*

*Polypodium interjectum*
'Cornubiense'
*(p.210) with…*

Carex fraseri
Cyclamen hederifolium
Dicentra spectabilis 'Alba'
Digitalis grandiflora 'Carillon'
Epimedium x versicolor
  'Sulphureum'
Helleborus orientalis
Hosta sieboldiana
Primula capitata subsp. *mooreana*
Pulmonaria 'Margery Fish'
Scilla bifolia

*Polystichum setiferum*
'Pulcherrimum Bevis'
*(p.96) with…*

Anemone nemorosa
  'Robinsoniana'
Bergenia 'Ballawley'
Carex elata 'Aurea'
Cyclamen coum
Galanthus plicatus
Geranium phaeum
Helleborus orientalis
Hyacinthoides non-scripta
Leucojum aestivum 'Gravetye
  Giant'
Narcissus 'Hawera'
Primula alpicola

*Pulsatilla vulgaris*
*(p.98) with…*

Anemone coronaria De Caen
  Group
Antirrhinum majus 'Scarlet Giant'
Aquilegia vulgaris
Astrantia major 'Roma'
Crocus tommasinianus 'Ruby
  Giant'
Epimedium grandiflorum 'Rose
  Queen'
Iris 'Blue Diamond' (Dutch)
Narcissus 'Thalia'
Primula 'Miss Indigo'
Tulipa 'Elegant Lady'

*Rodgersia aesculifolia*
(p. 174) *with…*

Acorus calamus 'Argenteostriatus'
Actaea rubra
Astilboides tabularis
Galanthus 'Magnet'
Hosta 'Big Daddy'
Lysichiton americanus
Osmunda regalis
Primula florindae
Rheum palmatum
  'Atrosanguineum'
Stipa gigantea
Zantedeschia aethiopica 'Green
  Goddess'

*Smyrnium perfoliatum*
(p. 100) *with…*

Achillea 'Credo'
Allium cernuum 'Hidcote'
Aquilegia 'Celestial Blue'
Cerinthe major 'Purpurascens'
Epimedium pinnatum subsp.
  colchicum
Erysimum cheiri 'Primrose Bedder'
Euphorbia griffithii 'Fireglow'
Geranium 'Johnson's Blue'
Gladiolus communis subsp.
  byzantinus
Iris x robusta 'Gerald Darby'
Limnanthes douglasii
Irises (purple Dutch)
Myosotis sylvestris
Tellima grandiflora

*Thalictrum aquilegiifolium*
(p. 102) *with…*

Alchemilla mollis
Catananche caerulea
Crinum x powellii
Geranium sanguineum
Gypsophila paniculata 'Bristol
  Fairy'
Helleborus orientalis
Iris 'Blue Magic' (Dutch)
Iris orientalis
Pulmonaria 'Margery Fish'
Tulipa 'Cantata'

## *Tulipa* 'Prinses Irene'
*(p.42) with...*

Ajuga reptans 'Catlin's Giant'
Anemone x hybrida 'Lady Gilmour'
Aster x frikartii 'Mönch'
Bellis perennis
Doronicum x excelsum 'Harpur
   Crewe'
Epimedium pinnatum subsp.
   colchicum
Eryngium giganteum 'Silver Ghost'
Erysimum cheiri (wallflower)
Erysimum linifolium
Euphorbia x martinii
Ferula communis
Glaucium flavum
Inula magnifica
Ligularia dentata 'Othello'
Lupins
Lysimachia ciliata 'Firecracker'
Myosotis (forget-me-not)
Primula 'Guinevere'
Rheum palmatum
   'Atrosanguineum'
Smyrnium perfoliatum

## *Tulipa sprengeri*
*(p.104) with...*

Ajuga reptans 'Atropurpurea'
Anemone x fulgens
Crocus goulimyi
Fritillaria acmopetala
Geranium cinereum var.
   subcaulescens
Hosta Tardiana Group
Iris 'Black Swan'
Primula Gold-laced Group
Primula 'Wanda'
Tellima grandiflora

## *Verbascum chaixii* 'Gainsborough'
*(p.176) with...*

Campanula persicifolia 'Fleur de
   Neige'
Eremurus himalaicus
Helianthus salicifolius
Hosta 'Wide Brim'
Salvia argentea
Senecio doria
Stachys byzantina 'Primrose
   Heron'
Stipa tenuissima
Tulipa 'Alice Leclercq'
Verbena bonariensis
Viola cornuta 'Eastgrove Blue
   Scented'

*Verbena bonariensis*
(p.212) *with...*

Canna indica 'Purpurea'
Crocus medius
Dahlia 'Grenadier'
Diascia 'Ruby Field'
Iris 'Professor Blaauw' (Dutch)
Nerine bowdenii
Patrinia scabiosifolia
Perilla frutescens var.
  purpurascens
Plectranthus argentatus
Salvia uliginosa

*Viola* 'Ardross Gem'
(p.106) *with...*

Alchemilla mollis
Ajuga reptans
Anemone blanda 'White
  Splendour'
Aquilegia vulgaris 'Nivea'
Arenaria montana
Aster alpinus
Carex elata 'Aurea'
Crocus sieberi 'Hubert Edelsten'
Geum montanum
x Heucherella alba 'Bridget Bloom'
Hosta sieboldiana
Iris 'Frans Hals' (Dutch)
Verbascum phoeniceum

*Zantedeschia aethiopica*
'Crowborough'
(p.108) *with...*

Astilbe 'Sprite'
Brunnera macrophylla 'Hadspen
  Cream'
Carex elata 'Aurea'
Lysichiton americanus
Osmunda regalis
Primula florindae

# Index

# Acknowledgments

## Author's acknowledgments

A book is a team effort and at Dorling Kindersley I have had a dream team: my wise editor, Pamela Brown, whose energy and determination never flag, and Peter Luff, the art director, whose clear eye has ensured that the book is not only easy to use, but elegant too. I would also like to thank the photographer Jonathan Buckley. He took enormous trouble to find the plants for the plant portraits and his skill has enhanced the book immeasurably. As always, I owe a debt to Christopher Lloyd and to Fergus Garrett, Great Dixter, Sussex, who grew many of the plants that Jonathan needed to photograph.

## Publisher's acknowledgments

With thanks to Hilary Bird for the index, to Tanis Smith for editorial assistance, and to Kelways Ltd for supplying peonies and irises for photography.

### Picture credits

The publisher would like to thank the following for their kind permission to reproduce their photographs: (Abbreviations key: t=top, b=bottom, r=right, l=left, c=centre)
**A-Z Botanical Collection:** Darryl Sweetland 80br; Ron Bass 160br; Dan Sams 172bl; Archie Young 176br; Adrian Thomas 200br
**Deni Bown:** 74bl, 138br, 154bl
**Jonathan Buckley:** 1, 2, 7tl, 10, 18, 20, 42br, 45, 46, 49, 57, 62, 67, 68, 72br, 73, 86bl, 97, 108bl, 111, 112, 119, 123, 124, 133, 145, 156br, 157, 164br, 168bl, 179, 183, 187, 190, 206bl, 207, 210bl, 218tl, 218tr, 223tl, 224tc, 231tc.
**Chelsea Garden Picture Library:** 166br.
**Neil Fletcher:** 92bl, 148bl, 151, 212bl, 221tl
**Mr Fothergill's Seeds:** 204bl.
**Garden Picture Library:** Brian Carter 24bl; Chris Burrows 98br; Friedrich Strauss 194br; Howard Rice 56, 84bl, 162br, 175, 200bl, 231tl; J S Sira 7, 120, 163, 225tr; Jerry Pavia 90br, 102bl; Mark Bolton 98bl, 203, 220tl; Mayer/Le Scanff 106bl; Mel Watson 58; Neil Holmes 28br, 32bl; Ron Evans 148br; Sunniva Harte 53, 88br, 115.
**John Glover:** 21, 28bl, 35, 39, 90bl, 107, 153, 170br, 221tr, 225tc, 227tc, 234tc.
**Andrew Lawson:** 3, 4tc, 9, 13, 16, 19, 34br, 38bl, 42bl, 50, 61, 72bl, 77, 78bl, 80bl, 82br, 82bl, 85, 95, 103, 109, 116, 127, 134, 141, 143, 144bl, 158br, 161, 180, 196bl, 198bl, 198br, 214l, 217tl, 217tc, 221tc, 225tl, 226tr, 230tc, 232tr, 234tr; Hadspen Gardens, Somerset 130.
**Clive Nichols:** 154br; Sir Terence Conran 212br.
**Photos Horticultural:** 26br, 30bl, 30br, 36br, 40bl, 86br, 94br, 104br, 106br, 174br, 202bl.
**Picturesmiths Limited:** 160bl.
**Howard Rice:** 94bl, 96bl, 100br, 146bl, 156bl, 208bl
**Bob Rundle:** 199, 217tr
**Harry Smith Collection:** 142bl, 150br.
**Thompson & Morgan:** 74br.
**Steven Wooster:** 24br, 32br, 38br, 174bl, 202br.

### Jacket Picture Credits
**Front jacket:** Flowers and Foliage: Carol Sharp r; Richard Freestone l.
**Back jacket:** Christine M Douglas br; Andrew Lawson cl.
**Spine:** Jonathan Buckley

All other images © Dorling Kindersley.
For further information see: **www.dkimages.com**